SCHOLASTIC

Key Stage 3
Years 7–9
Science
Revision Made Simple

Master science with ease

Answers included

SCHOLASTIC

Published in the UK by Scholastic, 2023

Scholastic Education, Bosworth Avenue, Warwick, CV34 6UQ

SCHOLASTIC and associated logos are trademarks and/or registered trademarks of Scholastic Inc.

© Scholastic, 2023

23456789 4567890123

A CIP catalogue record for this book is available from the British Library.

ISBN 978-0702-32681-3

Printed and bound by Bell & Bain Ltd, Glasgow

The book is made of materials from well-managed, FSC®-certified forests and other controlled sources.

MIX
Paper | Supporting responsible forestry
FSC® C007785

All rights reserved.
This book is sold subject to the condition that it shall not, by way of trade or otherwise, be lent, hired out or otherwise circulated in any form of binding or cover other than that in which it is published. No part of this publication may be reproduced, stored in a retrieval system, or transmitted in any form or by any other means (electronic, mechanical, photocopying, recording or otherwise) or used to train any artificial intelligence technologies without prior written permission of Scholastic Limited. Subject to EU law Scholastic Limited expressly reserves this work from the text and data mining exception.

Due to the nature of the web we cannot guarantee the content or links of any site mentioned.

We strongly recommend that teachers check websites before using them in the classroom.

Every effort has been made to trace copyright holders for the works reproduced in this book, and the Publishers apologise for any inadvertent omissions.

www.scholastic.co.uk

For safety or quality concerns:
UK: www.scholastic.co.uk/productinformation
EU: www.scholastic.ie/productinformation

Author
Danny Nicholson

Editorial team
Rachel Morgan, Vicki Yates, Bridie Begbie, Eric Pradel, Liz Evans and Aidan Gill

Design
Dipa Mistry, Andrea Lewis and PDQ Digital Media Solutions Limited

Illustration
David Rojas Marquez, scientific illustrator & PhD

Cover illustration
Freepik

Technical drawings
QBS Learning

Photographs
page 7: euglena, Ekky ilham/Shutterstock; page 7: amoeba, LebendKulturen.de; page 11: yeast cells, Rattiya Thondumhyu/Shutterstock; page 14: food pie chart, New Africa/Shutterstock; page 19: X-ray Sutthaburawonk/iStock; page 23: dandelion seeds, RomoloTavani/iStock; page 25: bee, Mr. Background/Shutterstock; page 30: camel, Wolfgang Zwanzger/Shutterstock; deforestation, Rich Carey/Shutterstock; page 31: Amazon Rainforest, Teo Tarras/Shutterstock; page 32: bricks, pardon06/Shutterstock; orange juice, Africa Studio/Shutterstock; balloons, Hayati Kayhan/Shutterstock; page 42: aeroplane, Jag_cz/Shutterstock; page 44: copper wires, Berents/Shutterstock, gold, Grasetto/iStock, bell, Graffixion/Shutterstock, palladium, RHJ/Shutterstock; page 45: sulfur, Sebastian Janicki/Shutterstock, bromine in a flask, RvKamalov gmail.com/Shutterstock; page 46: glowsticks, SetsukoN/iStock; page 46: cold pack, Andrey_Popov/Shutterstock; page 59: children on seesaw, brgfx/iStock; page 72: kettle, SolStock/iStock; page 83: woman with guitar, AboutLife/iStock

Contents

How to Use this Book 4
Periodic Table 5

Biology 6
Cells 6
Unicellular and Multicellular Organisms 7
Human Reproduction 8
Respiration 10
Breathing and Gas Exchange 12
Diet and Digestion 14
Skeleton, Muscles and Joints 16
Health and Drugs 18
Plants and Photosynthesis 20
Plant Reproduction 22
Relationships in an Ecosystem 24
DNA and Inheritance 26
Variation Between Organisms 28
Natural Selection and Biodiversity 30

Chemistry 32
Solids, Liquids, Gases and the Particle Model .. 32
Physical Changes 34
Atoms and Elements 35
Mixing and Moving Particles 36
Separating Mixtures 38
The Periodic Table 40
Types of Chemical Reaction 42
Metals and Non-metals 44
Endothermic and Exothermic Reactions ... 46
Acids and Bases 48
Metals and the Reactivity Series 50
Metals and Ores 52
Other Useful Materials 53
The Earth and Rocks 54
Carbon and the Climate 56

Physics 58
Forces 58
Speed and Relative Motion 60
Friction and Drag 62
Forces and Elasticity 63
Pressure 64
Non-contact Forces 66
Energy Stores and Energy Transfers 68
Work and Machines 70
Transferring Thermal Energy 71
Fuels and Energy Resources 72
Electrical Circuits 74
Magnets and Electromagnets 76
Properties of Waves 78
Light Waves 80
Sound Waves 82
Earth and Space 84

Glossary 86
Answers 91
Progress Tracker 94

How to Use this Book

This book has been written to help support science at Key Stage 3. The book will help you recap things you should have learned previously and to build on that with new subject information, followed by a chance to practise using this knowledge.

The book is divided into Biology, Physics and Chemistry and each of these subjects is broken into different chapters so you can choose which topic you want to practise. At the end of the book a progress tracker has been provided so you can see what you have done and what you haven't.

Answers can be found on pages 91–93.

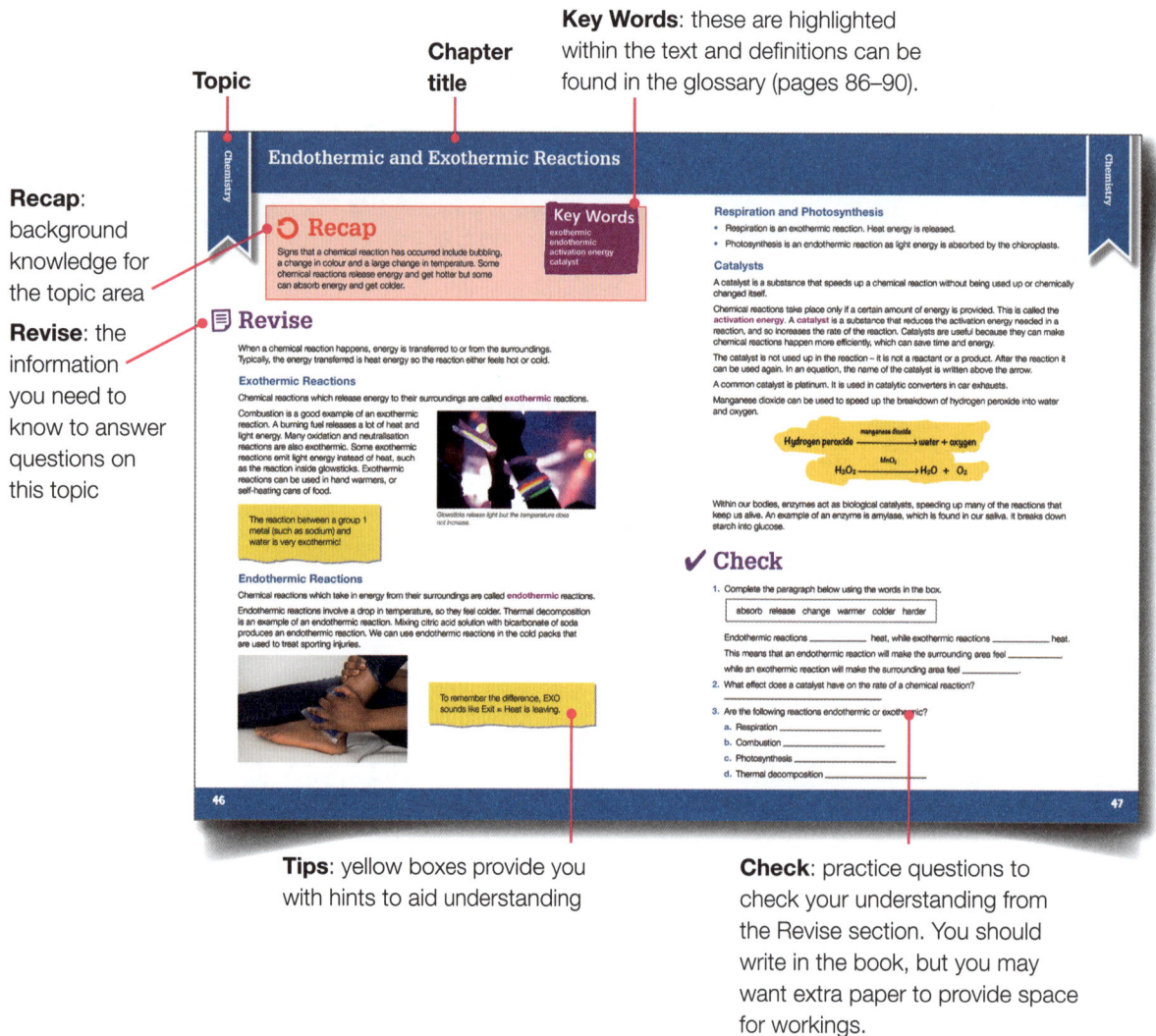

Topic

Chapter title

Key Words: these are highlighted within the text and definitions can be found in the glossary (pages 86–90).

Recap: background knowledge for the topic area

Revise: the information you need to know to answer questions on this topic

Tips: yellow boxes provide you with hints to aid understanding

Check: practice questions to check your understanding from the Revise section. You should write in the book, but you may want extra paper to provide space for workings.

Periodic Table

Key

- Atomic number
- Symbol
- Name
- Relative atomic mass

Colour legend:
- Non metal
- Alkali metal
- Alkali earth metal
- Transition metal
- Metalloid
- Noble gas
- Halogen
- Post-transition metal

Period	1	2											3	4	5	6	7	0
1	1 H Hydrogen 1																	2 He Helium 4
2	3 Li Lithium 7	4 Be Beryllium 9											5 B Boron 11	6 C Carbon 12	7 N Nitrogen 14	8 O Oxygen 16	9 F Fluorine 19	10 Ne Neon 20
3	11 Na Sodium 23	12 Mg Magnesium 24											13 Al Aluminium 27	14 Si Silicon 28	15 P Phosphorus 31	16 S Sulfur 32	17 Cl Chlorine 35.5	18 Ar Argon 40
4	19 K Potassium 39	20 Ca Calcium 40	21 Sc Scandium 45	22 Ti Titanium 48	23 V Vanadium 51	24 Cr Chromium 52	25 Mn Manganese 55	26 Fe Iron 56	27 Co Cobalt 59	28 Ni Nickel 59	29 Cu Copper 63.5	30 Zn Zinc 65	31 Ga Gallium 70	32 Ge Germanium 73	33 As Arsenic 75	34 Se Selenium 79	35 Br Bromine 80	36 Kr Krypton 84
5	37 Rb Rubidium 85	38 Sr Strontium 88	39 Y Yttrium 89	40 Zr Zirconium 91	41 Nb Niobium 93	42 Mo Molybdenum 96	43 Tc Technetium 96	44 Ru Ruthenium 101	45 Rh Rhodium 102	46 Pd Palladium 106	47 Ag Silver 108	48 Cd Cadmium 112	49 In Indium 115	50 Sn Tin 119	51 Sb Antimony 122	52 Te Tellurium 128	53 I Iodine 127	54 Xe Xenon 131
6	55 Cs Caesium 133	56 Ba Barium 137	57–71 La–Lu* Lanthanide	72 Hf Hafnium 178	73 Ta Tantalum 181	74 W Tungsten 184	75 Re Rhenium 186	76 Os Osmium 190	77 Ir Iridium 192	78 Pt Platinum 195	79 Au Gold 197	80 Hg Mercury 201	81 Tl Thallium 204	82 Pb Lead 207	83 Bi Bismuth 209	84 Po Polonium 209	85 At Astatine 210	86 Rn Radon 222
7	87 Fr Francium 223	88 Ra Radium 226	89–103 Ac–Lr* Actinide	104 Rf Rutherfordium 261	105 Db Dubnium 262	106 Sg Seaborgium 266	107 Bh Bohrium 264	108 Hs Hassium 277	109 Mt Meitnerium 268	110 Ds Darmstadtium 281	111 Rg Roentgenium 272	112 Cn Copernicium 285	113 Nh Nihonium 286	114 Fl Flerovium 289	115 Mc Moscovium 289	116 Lv Livermorium 293	117 Ts Tennessine 294	118 Og Oganesson 295

*Lanthanides (57–71) and Actinides (89–103) have been excluded

Relative atomic mass has been rounded to a whole number, except for Copper and Chlorine which have been rounded to one decimal place.

Cells

↻ Recap

All living things are made of cells. Animal cells and plant cells have a lot in common, but they also have several differences.

Key Words
membrane
nucleus
cytoplasm
mitochondria
cell wall
chloroplast
vacuole
diffusion

🗒 Revise

Animal Cells and Plant Cells

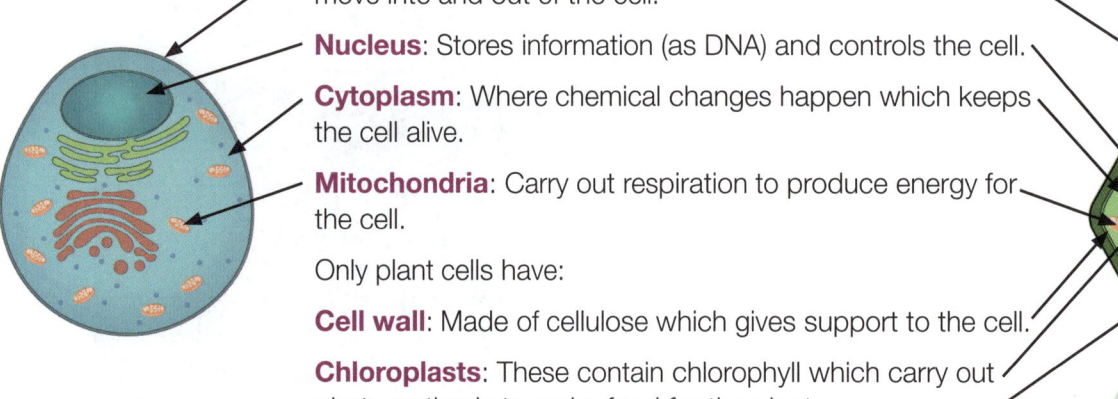

Animal and plant cells both have:

Cell **membrane**: Controls which substances are able to move into and out of the cell.

Nucleus: Stores information (as DNA) and controls the cell.

Cytoplasm: Where chemical changes happen which keeps the cell alive.

Mitochondria: Carry out respiration to produce energy for the cell.

Only plant cells have:

Cell wall: Made of cellulose which gives support to the cell.

Chloroplasts: These contain chlorophyll which carry out photosynthesis to make food for the plant.

Vacuole: which contains sap to keep the cell rigid.

Diffusion

To stay alive, cells need things like glucose and oxygen. They also need to get rid of the carbon dioxide they produce.

These substances get into and out of the cell through the cell membrane by a process called **diffusion**.

Diffusion is where a substance moves from an area of high concentration (lots of it) to an area of low concentration (less of it).

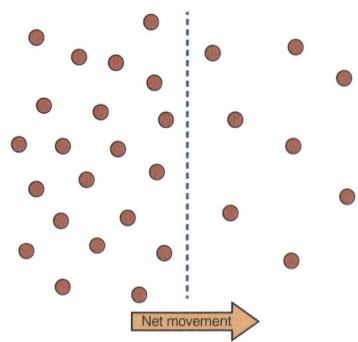

high concentration   low concentration

✓ Check

1. Name **two** structures that you find in a plant cell but not in an animal cell.
   _____ _____

2. Name the part of a cell that:
   a. Controls the cell: _____   b. Produces energy: _____
   c. Controls what goes into and out of the cell: _____

3. Complete the sentence: "Diffusion is the process where molecules move from an area of _____ concentration to an area of _____ concentration."

Unicellular and Multicellular Organisms

↻ Recap

Microorganisms are living things made of a single cell (**unicellular**). But the large living things we see around us are made of more than one cell (**multicellular**).

Key Words
unicellular
multicellular
tissue
organ
organ system
organism

Revise

Unicellular and Multicellular

Some living things are made up of just a single cell. This includes things like amoeba and euglena. These are called unicellular organisms. They have special adaptations to help them survive.

 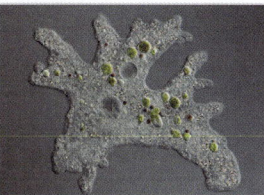

Euglena have a tail-like structure called a flagellum to help them swim.

Amoeba have a contractile vacuole which removes any excess water that gets inside them.

How Cells are Organised

Some cells have an adapted shape or features, for example, muscle cells can contract and red blood cells are thin and flexible so they can move through tiny blood vessels. Cells of the same type are organised into **tissues**.

Tissues are organised into organs to carry out particular jobs, such as the liver, skin or heart. Plants have organs too, such as leaves or roots.

Organs can be grouped together into **organ systems**. There are many different systems such as the circulatory system and immune system. Together, all these organ systems make up an **organism**.

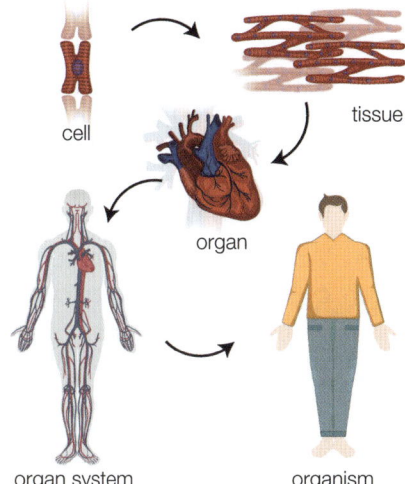

Using a Microscope

Cells are too small to see with the naked eye. Instead, we need to use a microscope.

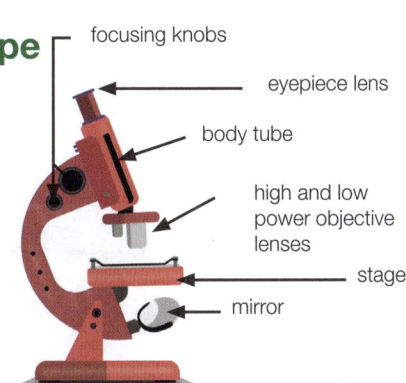

✓ Check

1. Give **one** way in which a euglena is adapted to live in water.

   _____

2. Complete these sentences:

   a. A group of similar cells come together to form a _____.

   b. Several organs can work together to form an _____.

3. Which part of a light microscope…

   a. do you look through? _____   b. holds the slide? _____

Human Reproduction

Recap

Male animals produce sperm and female animals produce eggs. When a sperm meets an egg, the egg is fertilised and will eventually develop into a baby.

Key Words
sperm cell
testes
egg cell
ovary
vagina
uterus
fertilisation
gestation
menstrual cycle
ovulation

Revise

The reproductive systems of men and women are very different because they have different functions.

Male and Female Reproductive Systems

- Males produce **sperm cells** in the **testes**.
- Females produce **egg cells** in the **ovaries**.
- During intercourse, the penis deposits sperm in the female's **vagina**.
- Sperm swim through the **uterus** (or womb) into the oviducts.
- When a sperm cell meets an egg cell the two cells join together, and **fertilisation** occurs.
- The fertilised egg develops into an embryo, a fetus and eventually a baby.

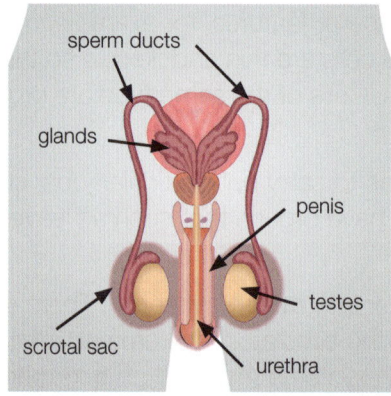
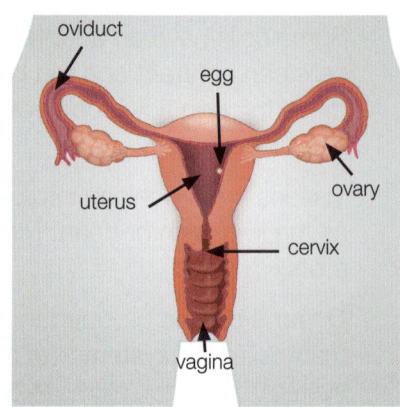

Gestation

During **gestation**, the embryo develops in the uterus (or womb).

- At around 4 weeks, the embryo's heart starts to beat. It has a brain, eyes, ears and legs.
- By around 9 weeks the baby is known as a fetus. It is about 25 mm long. Fingers and toes start to develop.
- At around 22 weeks, the baby's heartbeat can be detected. The lungs are starting to develop. It starts to kick.
- At 39 weeks the baby is fully developed and ready to be born.

While growing, the baby is connected through an umbilical cord to the placenta. This allows the exchange of food, oxygen, carbon dioxide and waste with the mother.

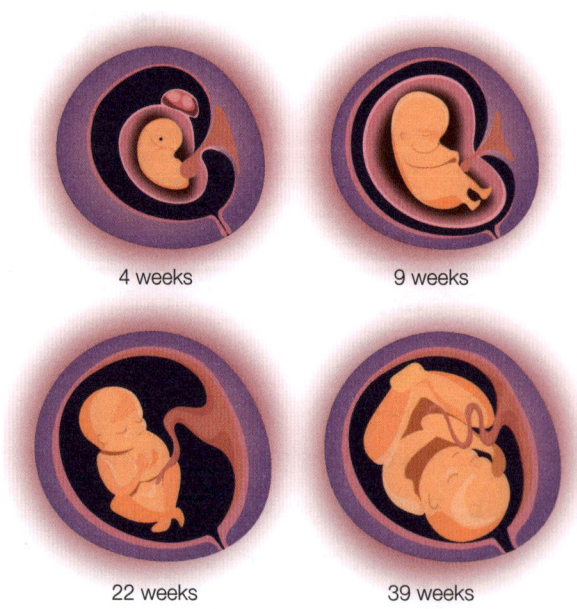

4 weeks   9 weeks
22 weeks   39 weeks

Menstruation

From the age of puberty, girls start a monthly sequence known as the **menstrual cycle**. Each cycle lasts roughly 28 days.

The menstrual cycle involves preparing the uterus to receive a fertilised egg. If an egg isn't fertilised then the egg and uterus lining break down and leave the body. This is known as a period or menstruation.

- Day 1: Period begins. The lining of the uterus breaks down and dead cells and blood pass out of the vagina.
- Day 4: The uterus lining starts to build up again. It develops into a thick spongy layer full of blood vessels.
- Day 14: An egg is released from one of the ovaries. This is known as **ovulation**. Fertilisation is possible from this point. The lining of the uterus is maintained.
- Day 28: If the egg has not been fertilised then the lining will start to break down and the cycle begins again.

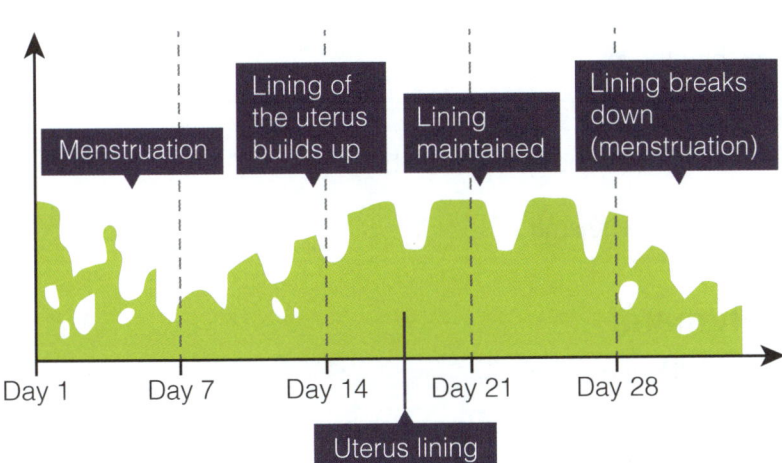

1. Which part of the male reproductive system:

    a. Makes the sperm? _____   b. Carries the sperm to the penis? _____

2. Which part of the female reproductive system:

    a. Produces the egg? _____   b. Is where the baby develops? _____

3. Name **two** things that the baby gets from the mother through the placenta.

    _____ _____

4. On which day of the menstrual cycle does the following occur?

    a. Period begins: _____   b. Uterus lining builds up: _____

    c. Egg released: _____

Respiration

Recap

Respiration is the process where living things release energy from their food. The fuel used in respiration is **glucose**.

Key Words
respiration
glucose
digestion
aerobic respiration
oxygen
anaerobic respiration
lactic acid
fermentation

Revise

All living things carry out a process called respiration. Respiration is the process by which living organisms release energy from glucose. This glucose comes from the **digestion** of food. The energy released is needed to power all the chemical processes necessary to stay alive. Respiration takes place in the mitochondria within cells. There are two types of respiration: aerobic and anaerobic.

Aerobic Respiration

- **Aerobic respiration** needs **oxygen**.
- The oxygen comes from the air we breathe in.
- Carbon dioxide and water are produced as waste products.
- The waste carbon dioxide is removed from the body when we breathe out.

glucose + oxygen ⟶ carbon dioxide + water + energy

Anaerobic Respiration in Humans

- **Anaerobic respiration** takes place without oxygen.
- In humans this can take place when not enough oxygen is available, such as whenwe are exercising vigorously.
- During anaerobic respiration in humans, **lactic acid** is produced.
- Anaerobic respiration releases less energy than aerobic respiration.
- Lactic acid can cause muscle pain, cramp and fatigue.

glucose ⟶ lactic acid + energy

Aerobic and Anaerobic Respiration in Humans

	Aerobic	Anaerobic
Uses glucose	Yes	Yes
Uses oxygen	Yes	No
Produces carbon dioxide	Yes	No
Produces water	Yes	No
Produces lactic acid	No	Yes
Amount of energy released	High	Low
Causes muscle fatigue	No	Yes

Anaerobic Respiration in Yeast

- Yeast (and some bacteria) can also respire without oxygen.
- They break down glucose into alcohol and carbon dioxide. This is called **fermentation**.
- We use yeast to produce alcoholic drinks such as wine and beer and also in baking bread. The carbon dioxide produced helps the bread rise.

glucose → alcohol + carbon dioxide + energy

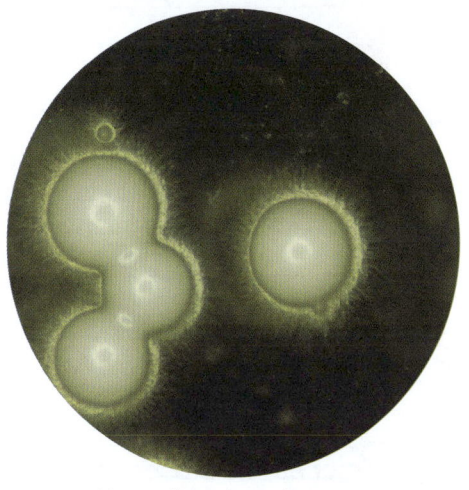

Yeast cells under a microscope

Where does Respiration Happen?

Respiration takes place in all living cells inside the mitochondria.

Cells such as muscle cells need lots of energy. They have lots of mitochondria to carry out respiration and supply the energy. Sperm cells also contain lots of mitochondria to give them energy to swim to the egg cell.

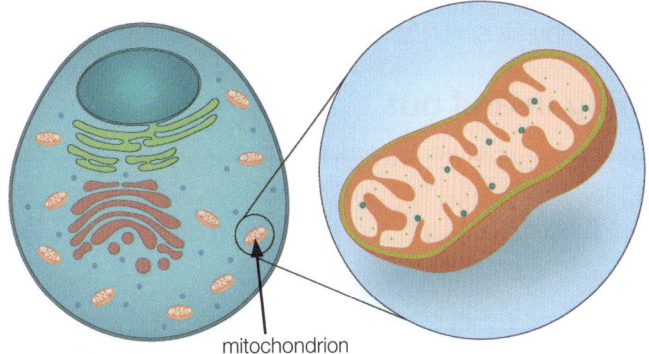

mitochondrion

✓ Check

1. What chemical is used in respiration?
   _____

2. In which part of the cell does respiration take place? _____

3. Aerobic respiration produces which two waste products?
   _____   _____

4. a. Anaerobic respiration in yeast produces which two waste products?
   _____   _____

   b. This process is also known as what? _____

Breathing and Gas Exchange

🔄 Recap

Breathing is the process where air is moved into and out of the lungs. While the air is in the lungs, oxygen moves into the blood and carbon dioxide moves out of the blood into the lungs to be breathed out.

Key Words
trachea
bronchiole
alveoli
diaphragm
gas exchange
cilia
asthma

📝 Revise

The respiratory system is made up of the lungs plus tubes such as the **trachea** and bronchi. It is responsible for moving air into and out of the body and exchanging gases with the blood.

The bronchi split into smaller tubes called **bronchioles** which end in tiny air sacs called **alveoli**.

Breathing in and out

The lungs are not able to move the air themselves. Breathing takes place because of muscles moving the ribcage and the **diaphragm** moving up and down.

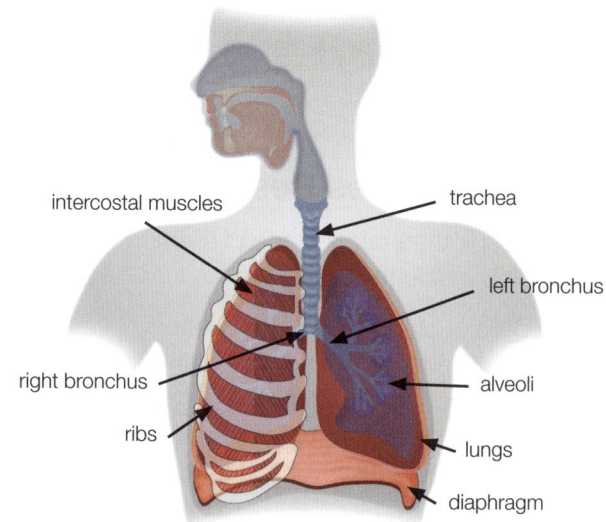

	Breathing in
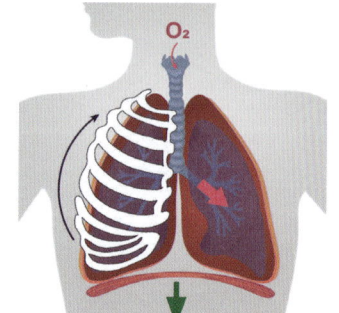	• Muscles move the ribs up and out. • The diaphragm flattens and moves downwards. • Lung volume increases, which decreases the pressure. • Air rushes into the lungs from outside.
	Breathing out
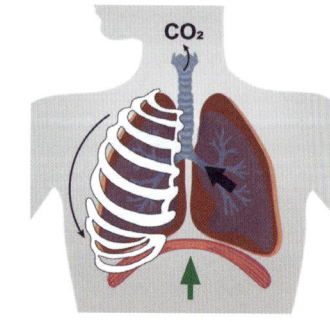	• Muscles move the ribs down and in. • Diaphragm domes back up. • Lung volume decreases, which increases the pressure. • Air is pushed out of the lungs.

The air we breathe in has more oxygen in it than the air we breathe out. The air we breathe out has more carbon dioxide in it than the air we breathe in.

Gas Exchange

Gas exchange takes place in the lungs. During gas exchange:

- Oxygen leaves the lungs and moves into the blood.
- Carbon dioxide leaves the blood and enters the lungs.

Inside the lungs are millions of air sacs called alveoli. Carbon dioxide and oxygen diffuse quickly and easily between the alveoli and blood because the alveoli:

- Have very thin walls
- Have a good blood supply
- Are moist to allow gases to dissolve and diffuse more quickly
- Give the lungs a large surface area.

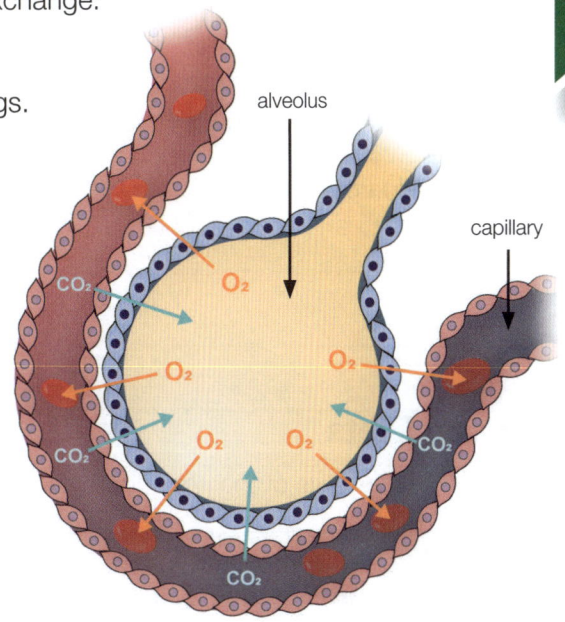

Red blood cells do not have a nucleus to allow more space for carrying oxygen.

Effects of Lifestyle and Disease

Over time, regular exercise can lead to an increase in the number of alveoli as well as the number and size of the blood vessels in your lungs which improves gas exchange. The cells that line the tubes of the lungs help keep the lungs clean by producing mucus. The lining cells have **cilia** (tiny hairs) which push the mucus out of your airways.

People with asthma have lungs that are very sensitive to certain allergens such as pet hair, pollen or smoke. **Asthma** can cause the bronchioles to close up, which makes breathing difficult. Medicines for asthma help to keep the bronchioles open.

Cigarette smoke can damage cilia in the lungs, causing mucus build-up and a persistent cough that further damages the lungs and makes breathing more difficult.

 Check

1. Complete this table to show what happens when you breathe in and out.

	Ribs	Diaphragm	Volume of chest	Movement of air
Breathing in	Move up and out		Increases	
Breathing out		Domes upwards		Out of lungs

2. What **four** features make alveoli very good for gas exchange?

   _____ _____ _____ _____

3. Give **two** ways that exercise can have a positive effect on our lungs.

   _____

   _____

4. What is the name of the process by which oxygen moves from the air into our blood?

   _____

Diet and Digestion

🔄 Recap

We get our energy from food, but we also need other nutrients to keep our bodies working properly. A balanced diet consists of all the right proportions of the different types of food. Our digestive system breaks down large molecules in our food so that they can be absorbed into our bodies.

Key Words
fat
carbohydrate
protein
vitamin
mineral
chemical reaction
fibre
scurvy
rickets
anaemia
enzyme
villi

📝 Revise

Balanced Diets

A balanced diet consists of the correct proportions of all the following nutrients:

Nutrient	Used for
Fat and **carbohydrates**	Energy. Can be stored in the body.
Protein	Growth and repair.
Vitamins and **minerals**	Used in various **chemical reactions** in the body.
Fibre	Helps undigested food move quickly through our intestines.
Water	Dissolves chemicals to allow chemical reactions to take place. 75% of your body is water.

Unbalanced Diets

Eating too much can lead to obesity. Eating too little can lead to starvation or malnutrition. Not getting enough vitamins and minerals in our diet can also lead to disease. A lack of vitamin C causes **scurvy**. A lack of vitamin D causes **rickets**. Not getting enough iron can lead to **anaemia**.

Energy Needs

Energy in food is measured in kilocalories or kilojoules. A typical 13-year-old boy needs about 10,100 kJ or 2414 calories (kCal) a day. A typical 13-year-old girl needs about 9300 kJ or 2223 calories (kCal) a day.

> What a dietician calls a calorie is what a scientist would call a kilocalorie. A kilocalorie is 1000 calories.

The Digestive System

The digestive system processes food after it is eaten. The large molecules inside our food are broken down by **enzymes** into smaller molecules so that they can be absorbed into the bloodstream.

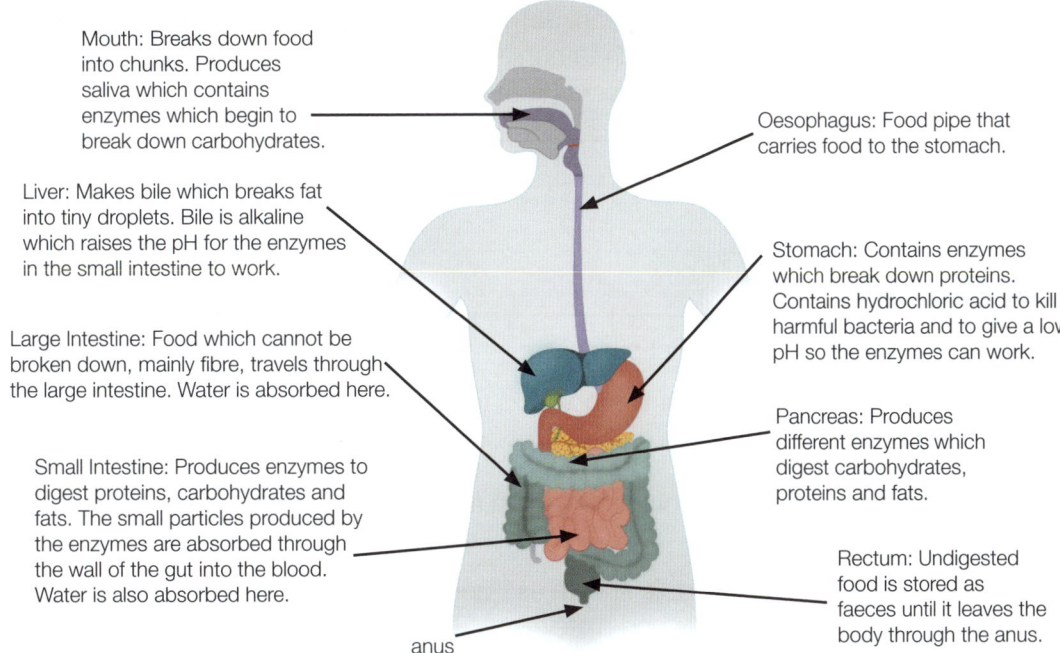

Mouth: Breaks down food into chunks. Produces saliva which contains enzymes which begin to break down carbohydrates.

Oesophagus: Food pipe that carries food to the stomach.

Liver: Makes bile which breaks fat into tiny droplets. Bile is alkaline which raises the pH for the enzymes in the small intestine to work.

Stomach: Contains enzymes which break down proteins. Contains hydrochloric acid to kill harmful bacteria and to give a low pH so the enzymes can work.

Large Intestine: Food which cannot be broken down, mainly fibre, travels through the large intestine. Water is absorbed here.

Pancreas: Produces different enzymes which digest carbohydrates, proteins and fats.

Small Intestine: Produces enzymes to digest proteins, carbohydrates and fats. The small particles produced by the enzymes are absorbed through the wall of the gut into the blood. Water is also absorbed here.

Rectum: Undigested food is stored as faeces until it leaves the body through the anus.

anus

Absorption of Digested Food

The small molecules of digested food pass through the wall of the small intestine into the blood (and are taken to where they are needed). This is called absorption. The wall of the small intestine is made up of millions of tiny finger-like structures called **villi** that give the wall of the small intestine a very large surface area.

Bacteria in our Guts

There are millions of bacteria living in your digestive system. These bacteria help to digest food. They can even help to prevent obesity, diabetes and some types of cancer.

 **Check**

1. What name do we give to the chemicals used to break food down into smaller pieces?
   _____

2. Give **two** reasons why the stomach contains hydrochloric acid.
   _____ _____

3. List **six** of the components needed for a healthy diet.
   _____ _____ _____
   _____ _____ _____

4. How do the villi help with absorption of food particles in the small intestine?
   _____

Skeleton, Muscles and Joints

↻ Recap

The human skeleton supports our bodies and allows it to move. Bones also protect some of our most vital organs. **Joints** are places where two bones meet or connect. Muscles attach to bones and allow our body to move. Each joint needs a pair of muscles to move.

Key Words
joint
ligament
cartilage
tendon
antagonistic pair

Revise

The Human Skeleton

The human skeleton has several different functions:

- It supports the body and gives it structure. It enables us to stand upright.
- It provides a framework that muscles can move.
- It protects important organs. The skull protects the brain and the ribs protect the heart and lungs.
- Many bones have a soft tissue in the middle known as bone marrow. This makes blood cells, such as red blood cells, white blood cells and platelets.

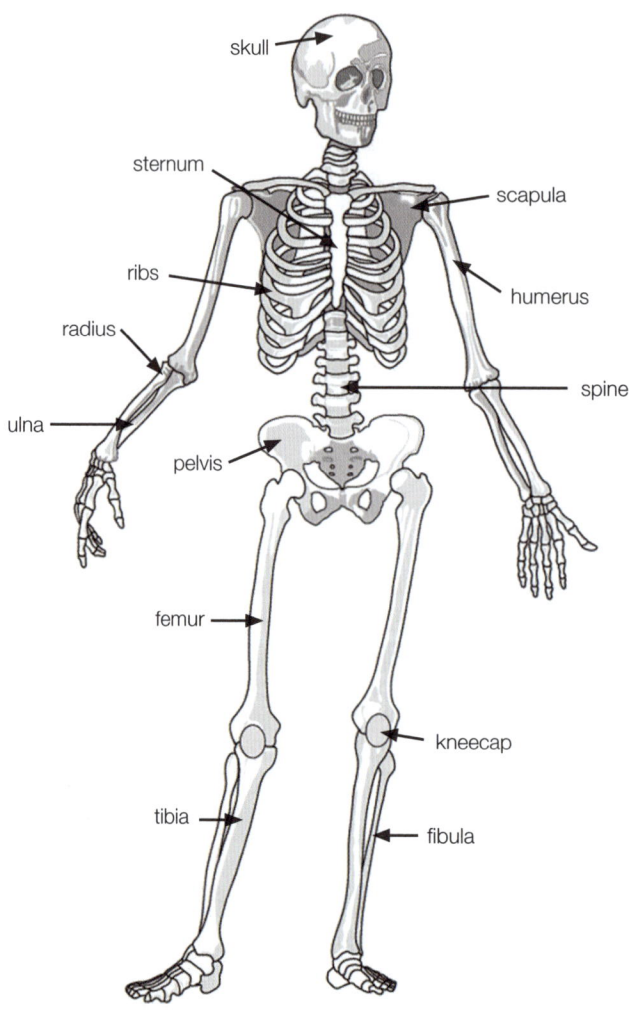

Joints

Joints are where bones meet. They allow the bones to move. Joints are held together by **ligaments** which join bone to bone. The end of each bone is covered in **cartilage** which is very smooth and allows easy movement. Joints are also filled with a fluid which lubricates them.

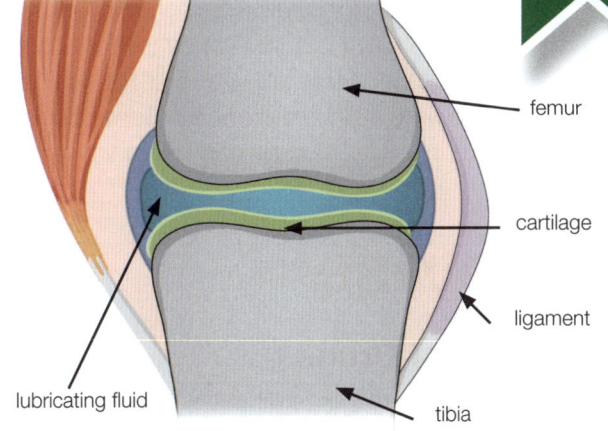

There are different types of joint, such as:

- Hinge joint: Bones can only move backwards and forwards, such as a knuckle or knee.
- Ball and socket joint: Bones can move in all directions, such as in the shoulder or hip.
- Pivot joint: This allows some circular movement, such as in the neck.

Muscles

- Muscles make our bones move.
- Muscles are attached to bones via **tendons**.
- Muscles work by contracting or getting shorter. This pulls the bone.
- Muscles cannot push, so another muscle is needed to pull it back.
- Muscles work in pairs called **antagonistic pairs**. One pulls the joint in one direction, the other pulls it in the opposite direction.

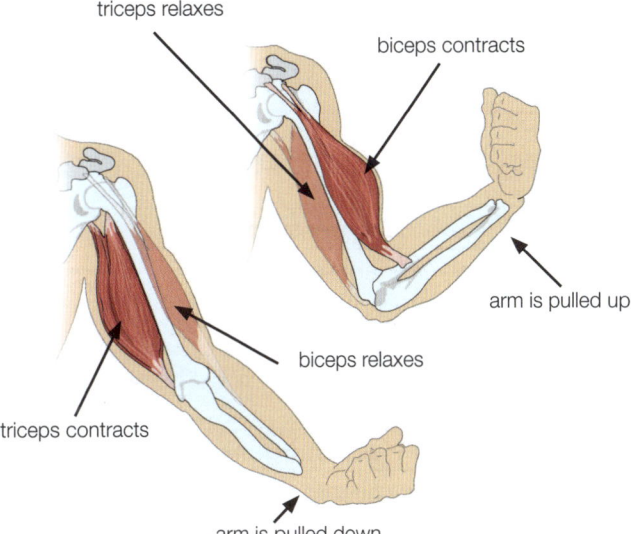

✓ Check

1. Give the **four** different roles performed by the skeleton.
   _____ _____
   _____ _____

2. What is the name of the tissue that joins bone to bone?
   _____

3. What is the name of the tissue that joins bone to muscle?
   _____

4. What part of a bone makes blood cells?
   _____

Health and Drugs

↻ Recap

A **drug** is a substance that affects our bodies in some way. There are legal drugs and illegal drugs. Drugs that can be used to treat diseases are called **medicines**. Some illegal drugs are taken for non-medical reasons. Drugs can be addictive and have unwanted side effects.

Key Words
drug
medicine
side effect
addiction
antibiotic
vaccination

Revise

Types of Drugs

Drugs taken for enjoyment, rather than as a medicine, are known as recreational drugs.

Some recreational drugs are legal and are commonly used, such as caffeine, alcohol and tobacco. They can have health risks and there are age restrictions on who can buy them.

Some recreational drugs are illegal, such as cocaine, cannabis, speed and ecstasy. They can have dangerous **side effects** and have serious health risks.

A side effect is an unwanted effect of any drug, legal or illegal. Some side effects are mild, for example, rashes, headaches and nausea, but others can be dangerous, for example, if your brain, heart or liver are damaged.

Depressants	Stimulants
• E.g. alcohol, cannabis and heroin	• E.g. caffeine, nicotine, cocaine and amphetamines
• Slow down the nervous system	• Speed up the nervous system
• Dangers include drowsiness and lack of coordination	• Can cause aggression and paranoia. Can also cause depression. Very addictive.
Hallucinogens	**Painkillers**
• E.g. LSD, magic mushrooms, ecstasy	• E.g. aspirin, paracetamol, ibuprofen
• Make you see or hear things that aren't there	• Reduce pain and inflammation
• Can cause confusion and flashbacks	• Can damage stomach lining or intestines
	• Incorrect use can lead to serious harm

Some drugs cause **addiction**, which means it can be hard for the user to stop taking the drug. They feel ill when they stop, and experience symptoms such as sweating, headaches, shivering and sickness.

Medicines

Antibiotics are chemicals that can kill bacteria that have entered our bodies. Antibiotics will not work on viruses.

Some diseases can be prevented by **vaccination**. This is when a dead or deactivated microbe (or part of a microbe) is injected into the body. The body makes antibodies to fight this microbe so we are protected if we ever meet it again.

> All medicines are drugs, but not all drugs are medicines.

Cigarettes and Alcohol

Two of the most common recreational drugs are alcohol and tobacco.

Both of these drugs are legal, but there are age restrictions on buying them. Both have serious health risks.

Tobacco

- Tobacco contains a drug called nicotine. Nicotine is very addictive.
- Nicotine is a stimulant - it speeds up heart rate and raises blood pressure. This can increase the risk of strokes, heart disease and heart attacks.
- Carbon monoxide and tar in cigarette smoke can cause breathing problems and make lung infections more likely.
- Tar and other chemicals in cigarette smoke can cause diseases such as cancer of the lungs, mouth, throat and blood vessels.

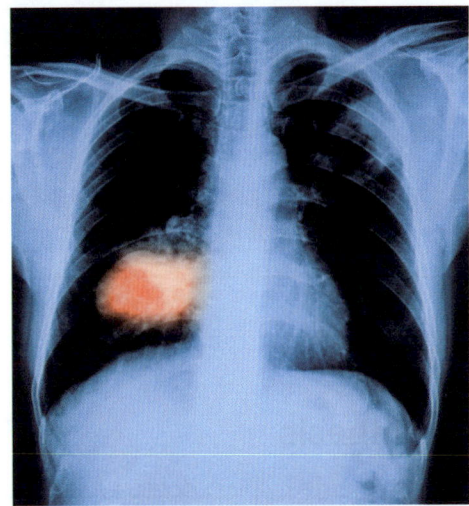

An X-ray photograph showing lung cancer in a smoker's lungs.

Alcohol

- Alcohol is a depressant - it slows down the activity of the brain.
- It is dangerous to drive a vehicle after drinking because it slows down your reactions and reduces coordination.
- It can also alter your behaviour and impair your judgement. It can be very addictive.
- Long term use of alcohol can damage the liver and the brain. It can increase the risk of strokes and heart problems.

If a woman smokes, drinks alcohol or takes other drugs while she is pregnant, harmful chemicals in her blood can cross the placenta and affect the fetus. This affects development and can lead to health problems in future.

✓ Check

1. What does the term 'side effect' mean?
   _____

2. Give **two** health risks caused by smoking.
   _____
   _____

3. What does addiction mean?
   _____

4. Give **two** long-term health risks caused by drinking alcohol.
   _____
   _____

Plants and Photosynthesis

Recap

Plants are able to make their food using energy from the sun. This mainly takes place in the leaves, which are adapted to capture as much sunlight as possible.

Key Words
photosynthesis
chlorophyll
palisade cells
stomata
xylem
phloem

Revise

Photosynthesis

- **Photosynthesis** is the process where plants make food.
- This takes place inside the chloroplasts inside plant cells all over the plant, but mainly in the leaves.
- Chloroplasts contain **chlorophyll**, a green chemical which captures the energy in the sunlight.

water + carbon dioxide ⟶ glucose + oxygen

Photosynthesis and respiration are the opposite of each other.

Plants photosynthesise only during the day. But they are respiring all the time, using some of the glucose they produce to release energy to keep the plant alive.

Leaves are Food Factories

Leaves are very well adapted for photosynthesis to take place:

- They are very broad and flat to give a large surface area for absorbing light.
- Cells near the top of the leaf (**palisade cells**) have the most chloroplasts as this area gets the most light.
- Inside the leaf are air spaces to let gases move around.
- Holes in the bottom of the leaf let the gases in and out.
- Veins inside the leaf carry water to the leaf, and take the glucose away to the rest of the plant.

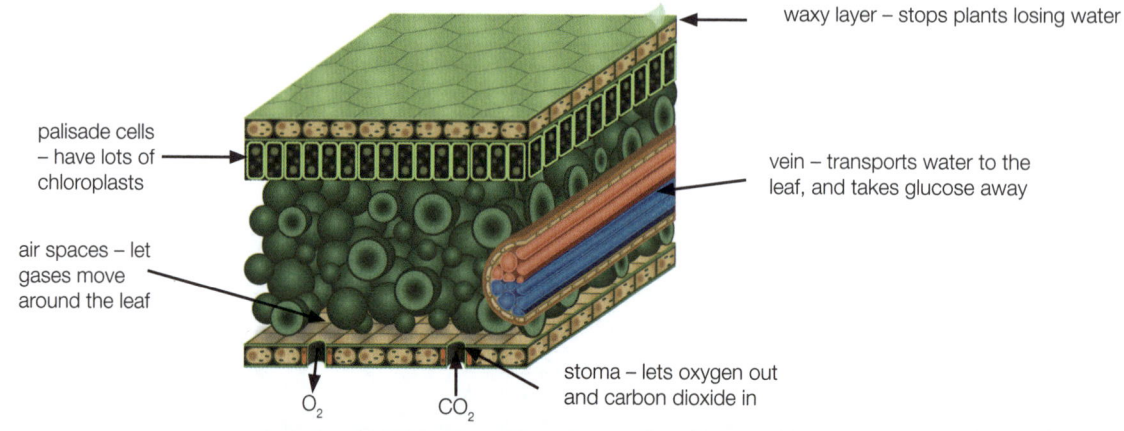

Getting Gases In and Out

- The underside of a leaf has many small holes called **stomata** (one hole is called a stoma).
- These holes allow carbon dioxide to get into the leaf and the oxygen to get out.

Transporting Water

Plant roots absorb water which they use in photosynthesis. They contain specially adapted cells that have a long finger-like part. This gives a large surface area to absorb as much water as possible. The roots also absorb minerals needed for growth and important chemical reactions.

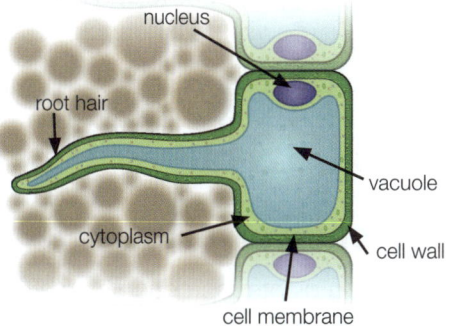

Plants have special tubes that carry water and minerals up from the roots called **xylem**. The tubes that carry water away from the leaves are called **phloem**.

Why is Photosynthesis Important?

- Photosynthesis by plants and algae is very important for almost all life on Earth.
- Plants provide animals with food. Animals eat plants or eat animals who have eaten plants.
- Photosynthesis produces the oxygen that humans and animals breathe.
- Photosynthesis stores energy by building up simple molecules (water, carbon dioxide) into a complex organic molecule (glucose).

✓ Check

1. Complete the word equation for photosynthesis.

   _____ + _____ → _____ + _____

2. Complete the table below.

Part of leaf	Function
Waxy layer	
	Transports water to the leaf. Takes glucose away.
Stomata	
	Where most of the photosynthesis takes place in a leaf. Have lots of chloroplasts.

3. Give **two** ways that photosynthesis is important to humans.

   _____

   _____

   _____

Plant Reproduction

↻ Recap

Reproduction is the process of creating new living organisms. In plants pollen joins an egg. This is called fertilisation. The fertilised egg then develops into a seed and, if the conditions are right, grows into a new plant.

Key Words
stamen
anther
carpel
stigma
style
pollination
fruit
dispersal

Revise

Structure of a Flower

Flowering plants reproduce by making seeds in the flowers. The seeds can then grow into a new plant.

The male parts of a flower are the **stamen**. These are made of an **anther** and a filament. Anthers produce pollen.

The female parts of a flower are called the **carpels**. Each carpel is made of a **stigma**, a **style** and an ovary. Ovaries contain the eggs.

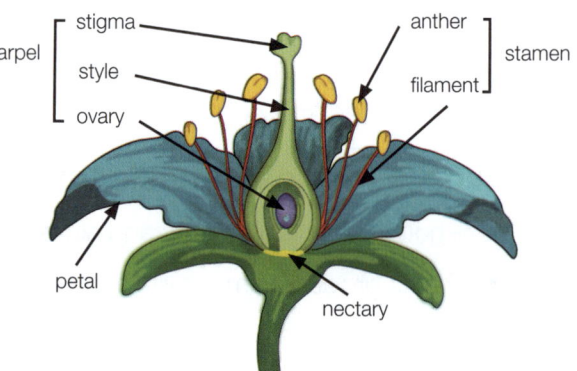

Pollination

Pollen is the male sex cell in plants. Eggs are the female sex cell. **Pollination** is the transfer of pollen grains from the anther of one flower to the stigma of another.

Some flowers are insect-pollinated, for example sunflowers. Insects carry the pollen from one flower to another.

- They have brightly coloured petals and a scent to attract insects.
- They may produce a sweet nectar that the insects like to eat.

Some flowers are wind-pollinated, for example dandelions. They drop pollen onto the breeze and the wind carries the pollen to other flowers.

- They do not need to attract insects so they don't produce a scent or nectar and their petals are not brightly coloured.
- Their stigma are large and feathery to catch pollen in the air.

Fertilisation

When a pollen grain lands on the stigma of a flower of the same species, a pollen tube forms, carrying the nucleus of the pollen grain. The pollen tube grows down the style into the ovary then into an ovule. The nucleus of the pollen grain joins with the nucleus of the egg – it is now fertilised.

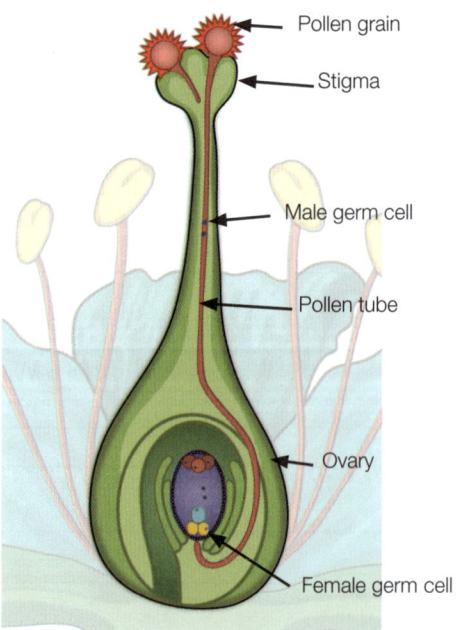

Pollen tube travelling down the stigma to the ovary and joining the egg.

Seeds and Fruits

After fertilisation, the ovule develops into a seed. The seed protects the embryo plant, and contains a food store. The ovary develops into a **fruit** around the seed.

Seed **dispersal** is very important. Plants have evolved ways of spreading seeds over large areas so that parent plants aren't competing with their offspring. Seed dispersal methods include:

- Animal dispersal: The fruit, such as corn or tomatoes, is eaten by animals and the seeds from the fruit pass through the animal's digestive system and come out in their waste. Some seeds have spiky coats which attach to an animal's fur and are carried away, such as burdock.
- Wind dispersal: The fruit have wings or parachutes which allows them to be carried on the breeze, such as dandelion or sycamore.
- Drop and roll: The fruit falls from the tree and rolls away, such as horse chestnut (conkers).
- Water: Some seeds can float on water, eventually reaching a new patch of land to grow on, such as coconuts.

Dandelion clocks have seeds which act as parachutes when they are carried by the wind.

✓ Check

1. Which part of the flower carries out each of these jobs?
    a. Makes pollen _____
    b. Contains the eggs _____
    c. Receives the pollen grains _____

2. Give **two** features that an insect-pollinated flower uses to attract insects.
   _____
   _____

3. Give **three** ways that a seed can be dispersed.
   _____
   _____
   _____

Relationships in an Ecosystem

Recap

An **ecosystem** consists of all the organisms in an area plus their environment. The organisms are **interdependent**, which means they all need each other to survive. We can show the relationship between how organisms eat each other using a **food web**.

Key Words
ecosystem
interdependent
food web
producer
consumer
food chain
bioaccumulation

Revise

Interdependence

Living organisms in an ecosystem are dependent on each other to survive. Mostly they rely on other organisms as food. We say they are interdependent.

Almost all life on Earth depends on plants. Plants use the energy from the Sun to produce food through photosynthesis (see pages 20–21). They are known as **producers**.

Animals cannot make their own food. They have to eat plants or other animals to get energy. They are known as **consumers**.

A **food chain** describes how each living organism gets its food in a particular environment. A food web contains lots of food chains. They give a better picture of the feeding relationships in the ecosystem.

Here is a typical food web. How many food chains can you make from it?

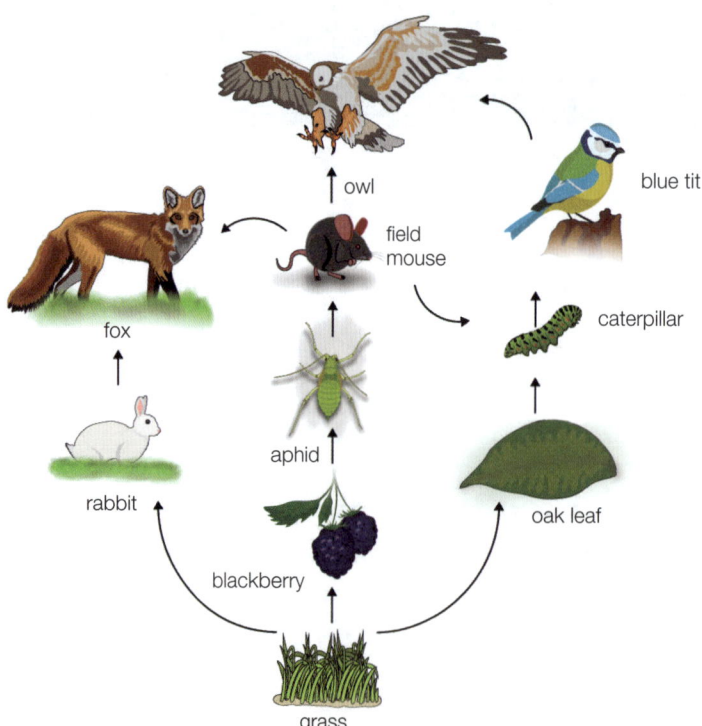

> The arrows show the direction of energy flow from one organism into the one that eats it.

Polluting the Environment

Sometimes dangerous chemicals (poisons) can get into an ecosystem, often because of human activity.

- Plants at the bottom of the food web absorb the poison.
- They pass it on to the animals that eat them. The animals are unable to excrete the poison, so it remains in their bodies and the level of poison builds up in them.
- Because each animal eats a lot of plants, they absorb large amounts of poison.
- Each level of the food web eats lots of the animals below them. The poison accumulates as it is passed up the food web.
- The top predators will be the worst affected and they can end up with very high levels of poison in their bodies. This is called **bioaccumulation**.

Human Food Supply

Humans are very reliant on other organisms for our food. We eat a wide variety of plants and animals and animal products.

Insects play a very important role in our food supply. They pollinate flowers so seeds and fruits can grow. These can be used as food for humans, or as food for animals that we eat. Without insects, we would struggle to get enough food for everyone. We should be careful when using insecticides to kill insect pests as they can also kill helpful pollinators such as bees.

✓ Check

1. Explain why food chains usually start with a green plant.
   _____

2. What do the arrows in a food chain/web show?
   _____

3. Here's a simple woodland food chain. Grass → Rabbit → Fox

   a. Which organism is the producer?
   _____

   b. Which organisms are consumers?
   _____

   c. Which organisms would be the worst affected by toxic material in this woodland?
   _____

   d. What word do scientists use to describe the build-up of toxic material in a food chain?
   _____

DNA and Inheritance

Recap

Parents pass down characteristics to their children such as eye colour and hair colour. Children are not identical to their parents and instead are a mix of the characteristics of both their parents.

Key Words
chromosome
DNA
gene
heredity

Revise

DNA, Chromosomes and Genes

- The nucleus inside your cells contains **chromosomes**.
- Chromosomes are made of long, coiled-up lengths of a chemical called **DNA**.
- DNA contains a special code which forms the instructions to build an organism.
- A **gene** is a short section of DNA which codes for a particular protein.
- Different genes (or sets of genes) control different characteristics, such as hair colour, eye colour, etc.
- Genes work in pairs, one from each matched pair of chromosomes. One gene is usually dominant over the other (which we call recessive).

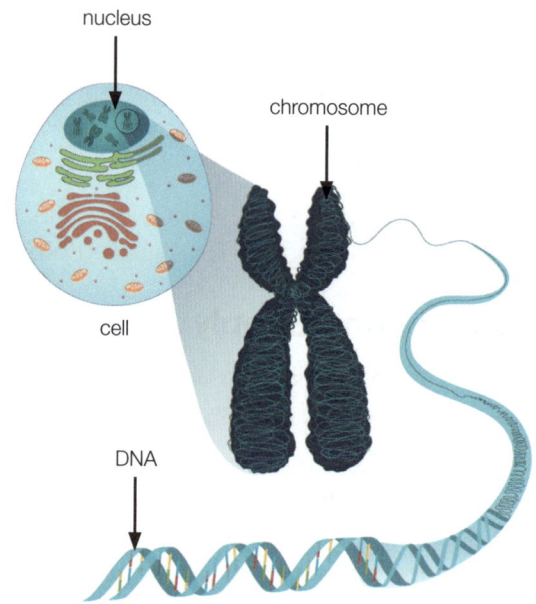

Inheritance

- Almost all our body cells have 23 pairs of chromosomes, making 46 in total.
- Sperm and egg cells contain only 23 chromosomes.
- When a sperm fertilises an egg, the chromosomes pair up.
- Each of us receives 23 chromosomes from our father and 23 from our mother.
- This mix of chromosomes means that we get a mix of characteristics from our parents.
- This passing down of genetic information from parents to children is called **heredity**.

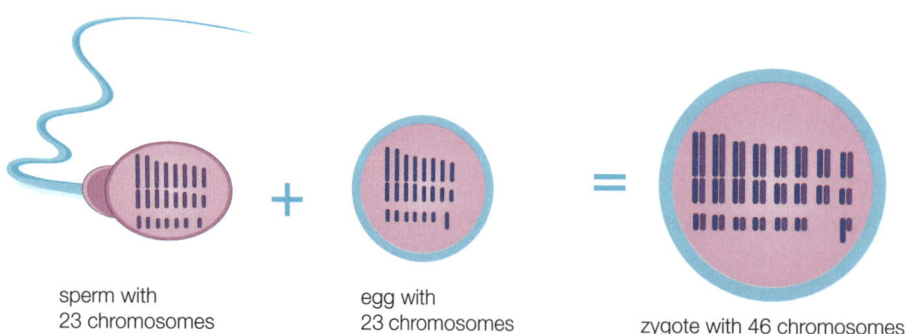

sperm with 23 chromosomes + egg with 23 chromosomes = zygote with 46 chromosomes

A Model for DNA

- DNA stands for deoxyribonucleic acid.
- Scientists worked for many years to discover the structure of DNA.
- In 1952, Rosalind Franklin took X-ray photographs which suggested DNA had a double-helix structure.
- Franklin worked with Maurice Wilkins who showed one of her photographs to James Watson and Francis Crick.
- In 1953, Watson and Crick used this information to build a model for the structure of DNA. They showed that DNA was made of two spiral chains wound together.
- In 1962, Watson, Crick and Wilkins won the Nobel Prize for their work on DNA.

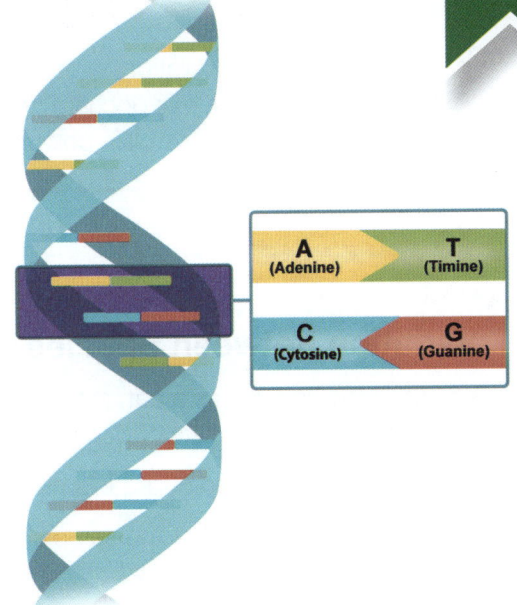

✓ Check

1. How many chromosomes are there in a body cell?

   _____

2. How many chromosomes are there in a sperm cell?

   _____

3. What is the name given to the process where genes are passed down from parents to offspring?

   _____

4. What is the name of the chemical that chromosomes are made of?

   _____

5. What is the name of the part of a chromosome that makes one protein?

   _____

Variation Between Organisms

Recap

Within a population, every individual is slightly different because they are a unique mix of characteristics from their parents. They may be different heights, skin colours or hair colour. This is called **variation**.

Key Words
variation
species
offspring
continuous variation
discontinuous variation
inherited

Revise

Variation between Species

- Living things such as a cat, a goldfish, a rose bush and a human look different because they have very different sets of genes. We say they are different **species**.
- A species is a group of organisms that can reproduce to produce fertile **offspring**.
- All pet dogs are part of the same species because they can breed with each other.
- Within a species there will be variation – not all dogs are the same size.

Types of Variation

- Variation between individuals within a particular species can be divided into **continuous** or **discontinuous variation**.

Continuous Variation

- Continuous variation is where the characteristic can vary over a range of different values.
- This includes height, weight, hand span, leaf area, length of tail, etc.
- Human height is a good example of continuous variation. It ranges from the shortest person in the world to the tallest, and every value in-between.
- On a graph, it makes a smooth distribution curve, or bell curve, with most of the readings in the middle and fewer people at either end.

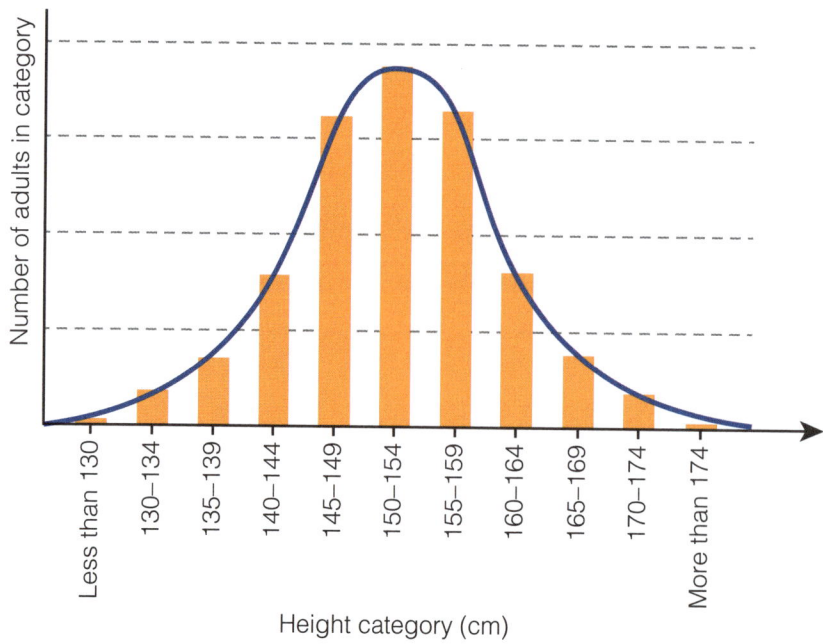

Discontinuous Variation

Some characteristics are limited to specific values:

- Blood groups are a good example of this. A person can be type A, B, AB or O. There is no gradual change between these values.
- A graph of this characteristic could not have a smooth curve or line of best fit. The data can be displayed in a bar chart.
- Other examples include whether or not you can roll your tongue, eye colour, fingerprints, and lobed or lobeless ears.

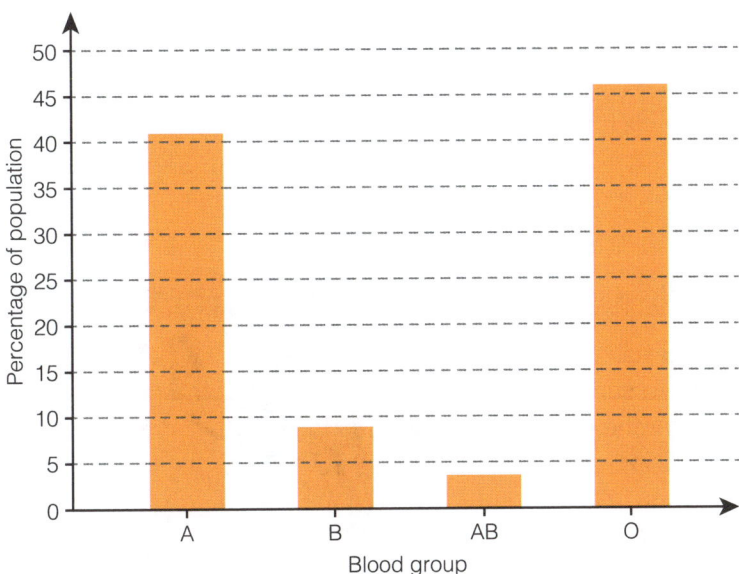

Causes of Variation: Inherited vs Environment

Variation can be caused by our genes (**inherited**) but it can also be affected by the environment. Variation could be affected by:

- Climate
- Lifestyle
- Diet
- Disease or accidents.

Identical twins share exactly the same genes but could look different if one has a healthier lifestyle or dyes their hair, for example.

 **Check**

1. Briefly explain the main cause of variation in humans.

   _____

2. Complete the table with the **two** types of variation and an example of each one.

Type of variation	Example

3. Give **two** reasons why identical twins might look different.

   _____

Natural Selection and Biodiversity

Recap

Organisms and plants have adapted to their environments over millions of years. Within every species there is variation. Having different characteristics might give some members of that species an advantage over the others and help them survive better.

Key Words
compete
natural selection
evolution
endangered
extinct
biodiversity
gene bank
conservation

Revise

Natural Selection

Organisms need to **compete** for the resources they need to survive and reproduce. These include food, water, shelter and mates. They need to compete with members of their own species as well as organisms from other species.

Within a species there is variation. Some characteristics might make an organism better at competing. It might be faster, stronger, have better hearing, etc. This makes it more likely to survive and reproduce, passing on the gene for the useful characteristic to the next generation. Over time the useful gene becomes more common in the population. This process is called **natural selection**.

The gradual change of a species over time, because of natural selection, is called **evolution**.

Camels have adapted to live in extreme hot and cold environments.

Changing Environments

The environment is not fixed and may change. For example, global warming may lead to areas becoming much drier than before, or seawater becoming more acidic.

- If the changes are very gradual, then organisms may adapt to the new conditions through natural selection.

- Large, rapid changes may mean that organisms are less able to compete for resources and reproduce. If a species cannot compete then that species may become **endangered**, or **extinct**.

- A species becoming extinct can affect other organisms in the ecosystem – if they rely on it for food or shelter, for example.

Extinction of species can cause problems for humans, if they are plants or animals we rely on for food, medicine and more.

- If pollinating insects such as bees become extinct then the supply of fruit and vegetables that we eat will be at risk.

- There may be plants in the rainforest with useful medical properties that become extinct before we ever discover them.

If deforestation continues at its current rate, rainforests will disappear within the next hundred years.

Biodiversity

Biodiversity is a measure of the range of different organisms in a habitat.

- Some habitats, such as a rainforest, are home to a huge range of species. Other habitats, such as a desert, have far fewer species living there and so are less biodiverse.

We can protect biodiversity through conservation and gene banks.

- A **gene bank** is a store of the genes of different species.
- For animals, we can store the sperm and eggs in freezers. If needed, these can be used to create new embryos.
- For plants, we can store seeds in seed banks for long periods of time. These can be planted to grow new plants.
- Gene banks may prevent extinction because if a species becomes endangered and its numbers fall, we could potentially breed more.
- **Conservation** includes protecting biodiverse areas and endangered species. It may involve putting some animals in zoos to keep them safe and organising breeding programmes with other zoos to maintain the population.

The Amazon Rainforest contains a third of the world's known plant and animal species, making it the most biodiverse place on Earth. It's vital that we take action to prevent the loss of this biodiversity.

✓ Check

1. What do we mean by biodiversity?

   _____

2. What would be stored in a gene bank for:

   a. animals? _____

   b. plants? _____

3. The process by which a gene or characteristic becomes more common in a population (over generations) is called _____.

4. What does extinct mean?

   _____

Solids, Liquids, Gases and the Particle Model

↻ Recap

Everything around us is made of matter. Solids, liquids and gases are three forms of matter. They behave in very different ways, with very different properties.

Key Words
state (of matter)
volume
density
compress

📋 Revise

Materials can be found in three different forms: solids, liquids and gases. We call these the three **states of matter**. Solids, liquids and gases have very different properties:

Solids

- Have a definite **volume**
- Have a definite shape
- Usually have a high **density**
- Are hard to squash
- Don't flow

Liquids

- Have a definite volume
- Change shape to fill their container
- Usually have a medium density
- Are hard to squash (**compress**)
- Can flow easily

Gases

- Have no definite volume, they always fill the container they are in
- Change shape to match the shape of their container
- Have a low density
- Are easily squashed
- Can flow easily

The Particle Model

All matter is made of tiny particles. The way that these particles are arranged is different in a solid, liquid and gas, and explains why they behave the way they do.

Solid

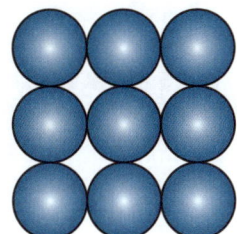

- Particles have the least energy
- Have strong forces of attraction between the particles
- Are held very closely together in fixed positions. Are able to vibrate
- Cannot move much, so shape and volume stay fixed
- Cannot be compressed easily because particles are already very close together
- Lots of particles in a small volume means solids are quite dense

Liquid

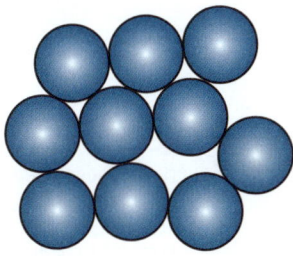

- Particles have more energy than in a solid
- Some forces of attraction between the particles
- Particles are still close together, so hard to compress
- Particles are able to move past each other, so shape of a liquid can change. Can flow and be poured. Volume is fixed
- Quite a lot of particles in a small volume, so still quite dense

Gas

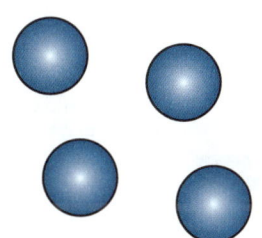

- Particles have the most energy
- Very weak forces of attraction between the particles
- Particles are far apart, moving in all directions
- Particles move fast, often colliding with each other and the wall of the container
- No definite shape and volume; will move to fill the entire container
- Big spaces between the particles mean they can be compressed
- Very few particles in a large volume mean gases have very low density

✓ Check

1. What makes a solid denser than a gas? _____
2. Complete this table:

	Solid	Liquid	Gas
Fixed shape?	Yes		
Can squash?		No	
Can pour?			Yes

3. Which state of matter:

   a. Has particles in fixed positions? _____

   b. Has particles spread far apart? _____

   c. Has particles close together but able to move? _____

Physical Changes

Recap

The three states of matter are solid, liquid and gas. A material that is solid can **melt** to become a liquid. A liquid can **evaporate** to become a gas. These changes of state are **reversible**.

Key Words
melt
evaporate
reversible
physical change
freeze
sublimation

Revise

Physical Changes

A **physical change** is when a substance changes state. Solid water (ice) can melt to become liquid water. Water **freezes** to ice. A physical change can be reversed easily.

Increasing the temperature (adding energy) will make a material change from a solid to a liquid and then to a gas. Decreasing the temperature (removing energy) makes a material change from a gas to a liquid and then to a solid.

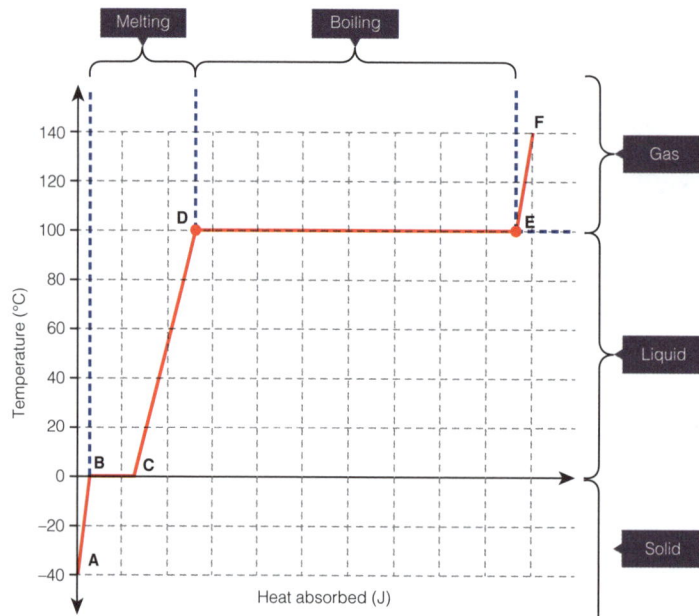

(**A–B**) solid ice is warming up.
(**B–C**) ice is at its melting point. The temperature does not increase during melting. The energy enables the particles to break the strong forces holding them together.
(**C–D**) liquid water is warming up. The particles move faster.
(**D–E**) water has reached boiling point. Particles now have enough to overcome the forces holding them together and become a gas.
(**E–F**) the water is now steam and continues to get hotter.

Sublimation

Some materials can change directly from a solid to a gas, without becoming a liquid. This is called **sublimation**. Solid carbon dioxide is called dry ice. As it warms it sublimes into carbon dioxide gas. Other chemicals that do this include ammonium chloride and iodine.

✓ Check

1. What temperature is the melting point of water? _____
2. What temperature is the boiling point of water? _____
3. Name the changes of state where:
    a. energy is added _____ _____
    b. energy is removed. _____ _____
4. What is the name of the process where a solid changes directly to a gas? _____

Atoms and Elements

↻ Recap

All materials are made of different chemicals. These chemicals are made of **atoms**. Some chemicals are made of just one type of atom, while others are made of combinations of different atoms.

Key Words
atom
element
compound
molecule

📄 Revise

Atoms and Elements

The smallest particle of matter is an atom. All substances are made up of atoms. An **element** is a substance that contains only identical atoms. An element is a pure substance that cannot be broken down into any other substances. There are 118 elements (see page 40).

Compounds

A **compound** is a pure substance that is made up of more than one type of element. The different element atoms are joined together. There are thousands of compounds, ranging from a simple compound such as carbon dioxide to complex one such as DNA.

carbon + oxygen → carbon dioxide
element   element   compound

Molecules

Atoms that are joined together are called **molecules**. Each molecule of carbon dioxide is two atoms of oxygen and one atom of carbon joined together. Each molecule of water is made of two hydrogen atoms joined to one oxygen atom.

hydrogen + oxygen → water

Elements like hydrogen and oxygen usually exist as pairs of the same type of atom joined together. We can draw this with circles to show the molecules.

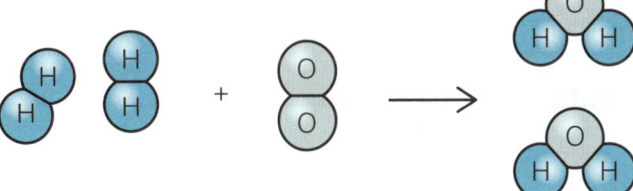

✓ Check

1. Substances that are made up of only one type of atom are called _____.
2. A _____ is a substance that is made up of more than one element that are chemically joined together.
3. A group of two or more atoms joined together is called a _____.
4. Water is made from atoms of _____ and _____ joined together.

Mixing and Moving Particles

↻ Recap

Solids, liquids and gases are made of particles. These particles don't just vanish when a solid dissolves in a liquid, or a liquid evaporates. The particles move and mix together. You can still taste them or smell them.

Key Words
dissolve
Brownian motion
diffusion

📄 Revise

Dissolving

Sugar doesn't disappear when you add it to a cup of tea. You can still taste the sugar, because it is still there. The sugar has **dissolved** – the sugar particles have spread apart in the water.

Solute: the solid being dissolved (e.g. sugar)

Solvent: the liquid it's dissolving into (e.g. water)

Solution: the mixture of solute in a solvent

Soluble: a substance able to be dissolved

Insoluble: a substance incapable of being dissolved.

When a solute has dissolved in a solvent, the liquid is called a solution.

Faster Dissolving

To speed up dissolving:

- Use hotter water: The particles move more and mix faster
- Stir it: This moves the particles more, helping them mix quicker
- Use finer sugar: Increases the surface area for the sugar particles to dissolve

Conservation of Mass

When sugar is added to water, no mass is lost. So, 10 g sugar added to 100 g water will weigh 110 g.

A can of regular fizzy drink will weigh about 35 g more than a diet version of the drink due to the dissolved sugar in it. Grab a can and check!

Moving Gases

Brownian Motion

Brownian motion is the random movement of particles in a liquid or gas. It was discovered in 1827 by Robert Brown. Large particles (such as smoke) can be moved with Brownian motion by fast moving, smaller, lighter particles such as air.

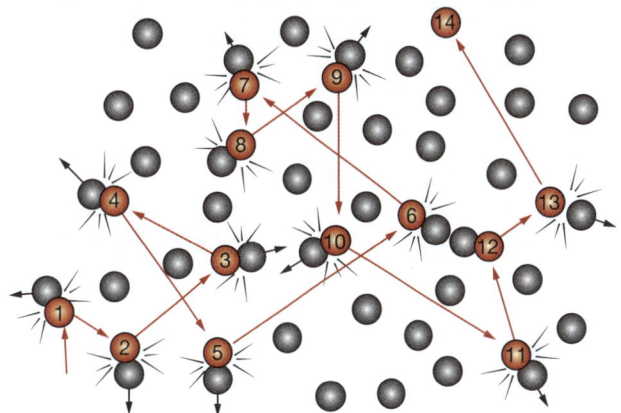

Diffusion

Spray some perfume in one corner of a room and eventually the smell will travel all over the room. This is because the Brownian motion of the particles in a gas or liquid mean that eventually the particles spread out or **diffuse**. The particles collide randomly and spread out from an area of high concentration to an area of low concentration.

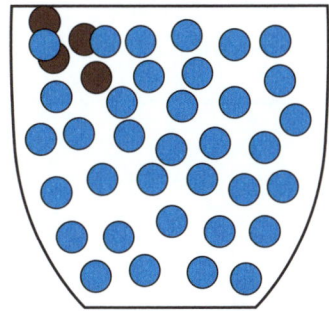 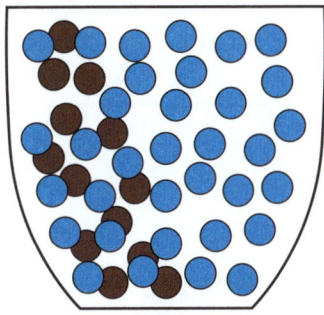 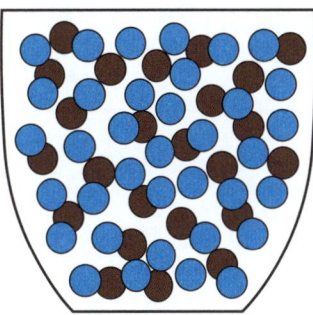

1. Highly concentrated coffee molecules enter the cup of hot water.
2. Coffee molecules begin to spread out in between the water molecules.
3. Coffee molecules are now in a lower concentration than they started in.

✔ Check

1. 20 g of salt is dissolved in 200 g of water. What is the mass of the solution? _____
2. Give **three** ways to make sugar dissolve quicker.

   _____   _____

   _____

3. Complete this sentence to explain what happens when a stink bomb is let off:

   The smell particles move from an area of _____ concentration to an area of _____ concentration to fill the room. This process is called _____.

4. What do we call the random motion of particles in a gas or liquid?

   _____

Separating Mixtures

> ## ↻ Recap
> Pure substances are made of only one type of element or compound. A mixture is a substance that contains several elements or compounds which are not chemically joined to each other.

Key Words
distillation
chromatography

Revise

A pure substance is one that contains only one type of atom or compound. A mixture is an impure substance. It contains two or more different substances that are not chemically joined together. It's possible to separate them easily using different physical methods.

Examples of mixtures include seawater, a sugary drink and air.

Filtration and Evaporation

Rock salt is a mixture of salt and sand. Salt is soluble, because it dissolves in water. Sand is insoluble, because it won't dissolve in water. To separate the rock salt, use this process:

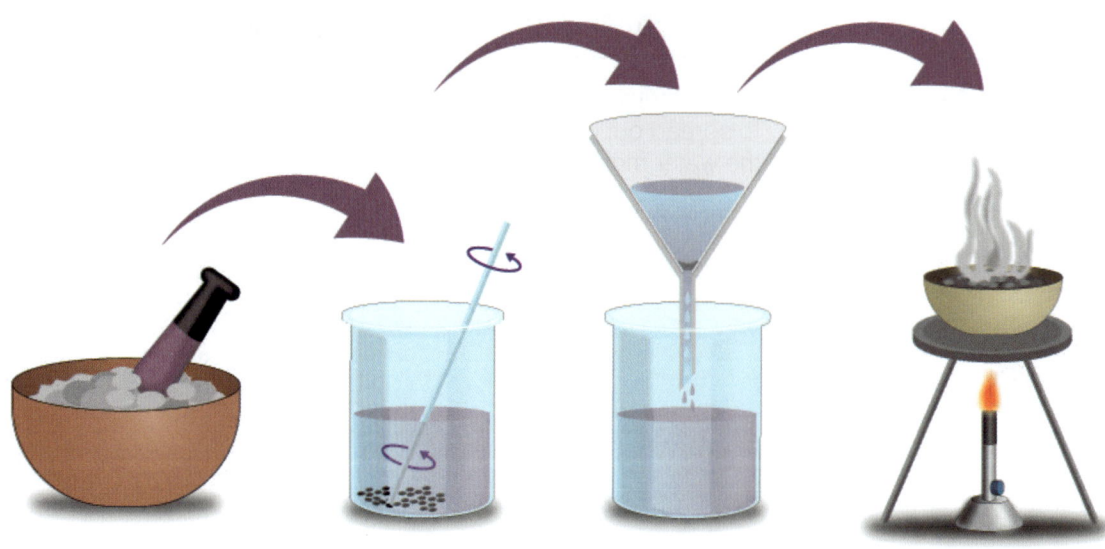

Grinding: Grind up the rock salt in a pestle and mortar.

Dissolving: Add the powder to a beaker of water and stir. This will dissolve the salt and leave the sand.

Filtering: Pour the contents of the beaker through filter paper in a funnel. The dissolved salt will pass through the tiny holes in the paper. The larger grains of sand will remain on the paper.

Evaporating: Heat the salt solution in an evaporating dish to evaporate off the water. The salt will crystallise and leave solid salt crystals in the dish.

Distillation

Distillation can be used to get pure water from seawater.

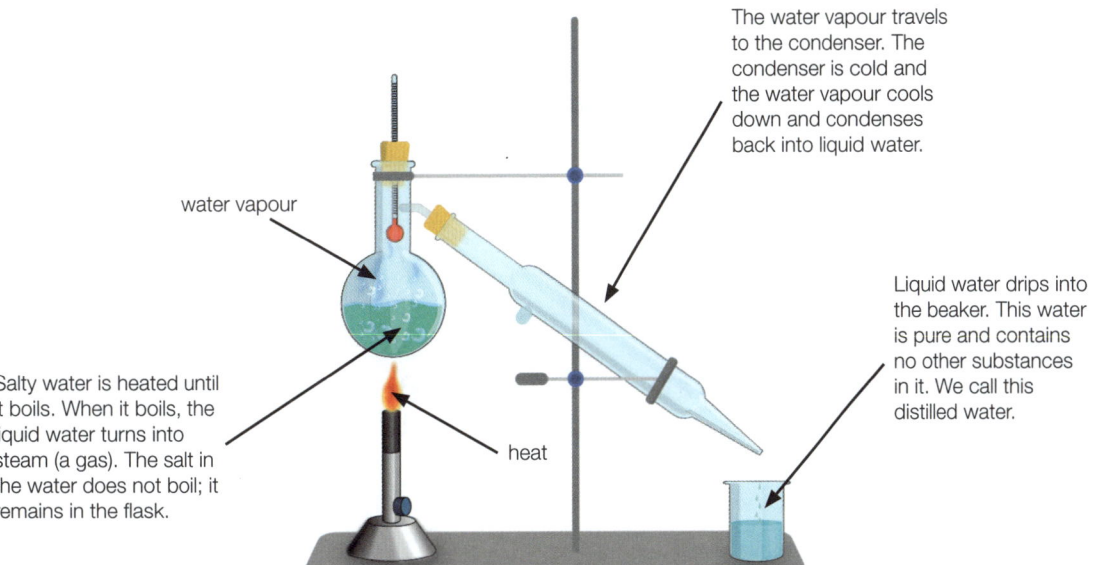

The water vapour travels to the condenser. The condenser is cold and the water vapour cools down and condenses back into liquid water.

water vapour

Liquid water drips into the beaker. This water is pure and contains no other substances in it. We call this distilled water.

Salty water is heated until it boils. When it boils, the liquid water turns into steam (a gas). The salt in the water does not boil; it remains in the flask.

heat

Chromatography

The ink in a pen is often a mixture of ink of several different colours. To separate them, we can use **chromatography**.

1. Put different inks along the edge of a piece of filter paper, along a marked pencil line.

2. Dip the filter paper into a solvent (water).

3. As the solvent moves up the paper, it carries the ink with it. Different inks will travel through paper at different rates. The more soluble the ink, the further it will travel.

✓ Check

1. Which process would you use:

    a. To get clean water from muddy water? _____

    b. To see if a sweet is coloured by one dye or a mixture of dyes? _____

    c. To get the sugar out of a glass of sugary water? _____

2. What are names of the four steps to extract salt from rock salt?

    _____ _____
    _____ _____

3. Distilled water is pure. What does 'pure' mean?

    _____

The Periodic Table

Recap

An element is a pure substance that cannot be broken down any further. There are 118 known elements. Scientists can sort and group them based on their structure and properties.

Key Words
atomic number
group
period

Revise

The Periodic Table

All 118 known elements can be arranged in a chart called the Periodic Table. This chart was developed by Dmitri Mendeleev in 1869. In it, elements are ordered by their **atomic number** – the number of protons in the nucleus of the atom.

Each column is called a **group**. Each element in the group shares similar physical and chemical properties. Each row is called a **period**. The periodic table also groups elements into metals, and non-metals.

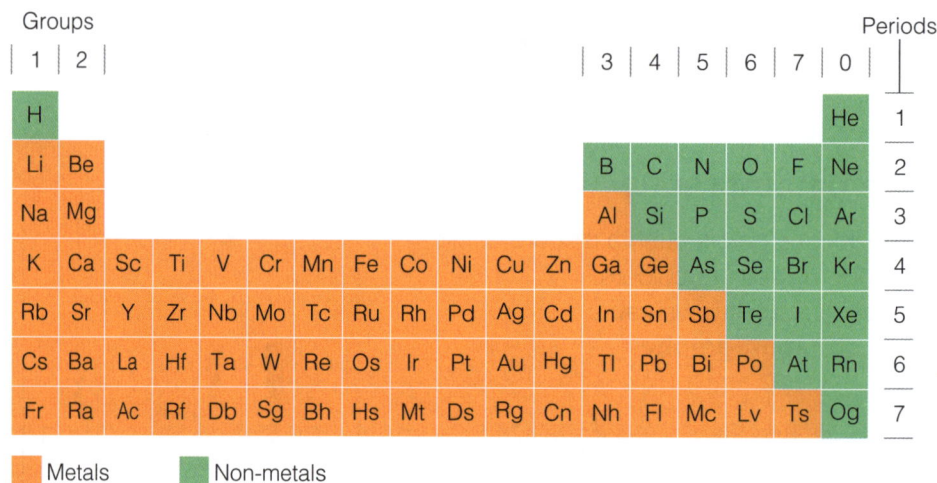

Making Predictions

Scientists can use the periodic table to predict the properties of elements in a group based on the properties of other elements in the same group, and patterns of behaviour down a group.

Group 1 contains soft, shiny metals such as lithium and sodium.
All group 1 metals react with water. The metals become more reactive as you go down the group.

Group 7 contains the halogen gases such as chlorine and fluorine. These gases become less reactive as you move down the group.

Group 0 are all gases such as helium and neon. They are all very unreactive. We call these the noble gases.

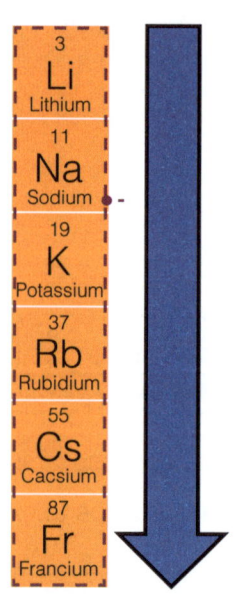

Reactivity increases down the group

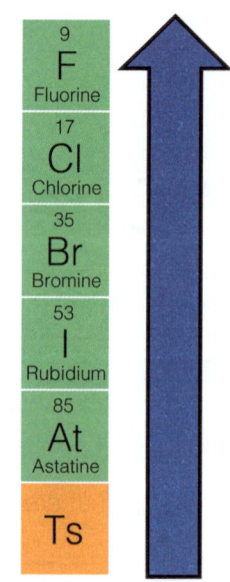

Reactivity increases up the group

Symbols and Formulae

Every element in the periodic table has a unique chemical symbol.

H = Hydrogen   Li = Lithium   C = Carbon

O = Oxygen   Pb = Lead   Zn = Zinc

The symbol always starts with a capital letter. Any additional letters are always lower case.

When elements are chemically combined to form a compound, the symbols are combined to represent the chemical formula for the compound.

Water can be represented as H_2O. The small number 2 shows that there are two hydrogen atoms joined to one oxygen atom:

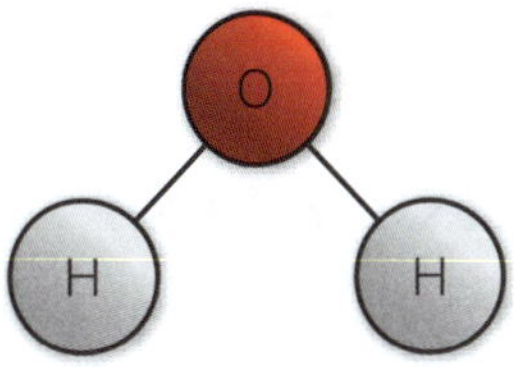

The symbol for sodium is Na and the symbol for chlorine is Cl. Table salt, which is sodium chloride, has the formula NaCl.

The chemical formula for glucose is $C_6H_{12}O_6$. A molecule of glucose contains 6 carbon atoms, 12 hydrogen atoms and 6 oxygen atoms.

Properties of Water

Compounds can have very different properties from the elements they are made from. For example, hydrogen and oxygen are both flammable gases. Water is non-flammable and is a liquid at room temperature. Unlike most substances, water becomes less dense when it turns from a liquid to a solid, which explains the reason why ice floats.

✓ Check

1. Element X is a member of group 1. Give **three** things you can predict about how element X looks and behaves.

   _____
   _____
   _____

2. Element Y is in group 7. It is found below chlorine. Is element Y more or less reactive than chlorine? _____

3. Element Z is found on the far right-hand side of the Periodic Table. Is element Z a metal or a non-metal? _____

4. Methane has the formula CH_4. Complete this sentence:

   Methane is made from one _____ atom and _____ hydrogen atoms.

Types of Chemical Reaction

🔄 Recap

Chemical changes are different from physical changes. Chemical changes result in the formation of new chemical compounds and are not that easy to reverse.

Key Words
reactant
product
chemical reaction
combustion
hydrocarbon
thermal decomposition
oxidation

Revise

Chemical Changes

Before a reaction, chemicals are called **reactants**, and after a reaction they are called **products**. In a chemical change, new chemicals are made. The atoms in the reactants rearrange to form the new products. The total number of atoms does not change; they just rearrange into different compounds.

Evidence of a **chemical reaction** includes a large temperature change, the emergence of bubbles or a colour change.

Conservation of Mass

The total mass before and after a reaction does not change. The mass of reactants is the same as the mass of products.

For example, adding zinc to copper sulphate solution. The zinc and copper sulphate will change colour as they react, but the overall mass will stay the same.

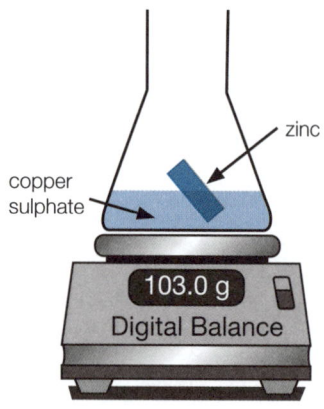

Combustion

Combustion is burning a material in oxygen. During combustion a fuel reacts with oxygen to release energy. Three things are needed for combustion to happen: fuel, heat and oxygen.

Fuels such as wood, coal and petrol contain chemicals called **hydrocarbons**. They contain only hydrogen and carbon.

hydrocarbon + oxygen → carbon dioxide + water + energy

Hydrocarbons are highly combustible and the main source of energy in the world. Jet fuel is derived from a hydrocarbon.

Thermal Decomposition

Thermal decomposition is when a compound breaks down into other substances when heated. These substances could be compounds, or could be elements. There is only one reactant, but it is still a chemical change.

Sodium hydrogen carbonate breaks down to sodium carbonate, water and carbon dioxide when heated.

Copper carbonate breaks down to copper oxide and carbon dioxide when heated. Copper carbonate is green. Copper oxide is black.

copper carbonate ⟶ copper oxide + carbon dioxide
$CuCO_3 \rightarrow CuO + CO_2$

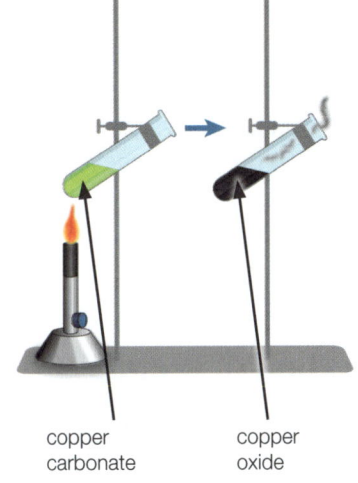

copper carbonate   copper oxide

Oxidation

In an **oxidation** reaction, an element or compound gains oxygen atoms. Combustion is an example of an oxidation reaction. Burning a hydrocarbon such as methane produces carbon dioxide and water. Both the hydrogen and the carbon atoms gain oxygen atoms.

methane ⟶ carbon dioxide + water

Magnesium reacts with oxygen to produce magnesium oxide:

magnesium + oxygen ⟶ magnesium oxide
$Mg + O_2 \rightarrow MgO$

Magnesium when burning gives off a very bright light, so don't look directly at it!

Rusting is also an example of oxidation. Iron gains oxygen to become iron oxide:

iron + oxygen ⟶ iron oxide

The opposite of oxidation, where oxygen is lost, is called reduction.

✓ Check

1. Copper metal is heated in a Bunsen flame in air. The copper turns black.

    a. What is the name of this type of chemical reaction? _____

    b. What compound has been produced? _____

    c. Write a word equation for this reaction. _____

2. What products are formed when a metal carbonate breaks down by thermal decomposition?
   _____

3. What **three** things are needed for combustion to occur?
   _____ _____ _____

Metals and Non-metals

> ## ↻ Recap
>
> Elements can be divided into metals and non-metals. Metals can be found on the left and middle of the periodic table, and non-metals on the right. They have quite different properties.

Key Words
conductor
malleable
ductile
alloy
insulator

🗏 Revise

Properties of Metals

Metals include elements such as gold, silver, iron, aluminium and magnesium. They have many properties in common:

Metals Conduct Electricity

- Metals are good **conductors** of electricity.
- Metals contain some electrons which are able to move freely.
- These electrons can carry an electric charge along a piece of metal.

Metals Conduct Thermal Energy

- Metals are good at conducting thermal (heat) energy from a hot place to a cold place.
- The hot particles vibrate greatly and pass these vibrations along to neighbouring particles.
- Free electrons in the metal also help to transfer heat energy.

Metals are Malleable and Ductile

- **Malleable** – they can be beaten into shapes or made into thin sheets.
- **Ductile** – they can be drawn into thin wires.

Metals are Shiny

- When metals are freshly cut or polished, they are good at reflecting light. This makes them look shiny.

Metals are Strong

- Metals have very strong bonds between their atoms which give them a very high tensile strength.
- This makes them very good for cables, for armour and for use in construction.

Most Metals are Solids

- They have high melting and boiling points because their atoms are joined with strong bonds.
- It takes a lot of energy to break these bonds and melt a metal.
- Mercury is the only metal that is a liquid at room temperature.

Some Metals are Magnetic

- Metals such as iron, cobalt and nickel are magnetic.
- **Alloys** made with these metals, such as steel, can also be magnetic.

Metals form Alloys

- Metals can be mixed to form alloys with different properties.
- Common alloys include brass, bronze and steel.

Metals are Sonorous

- Metals make a ringing sound when hit. It's why we use metals in musical instruments like bells, triangles and cymbals

Properties of Non-metals

Non-metals include elements such as oxygen, helium, nitrogen, sulfur and carbon.

Non-metals have Low Melting and Boiling Points

- The forces between the atoms are very weak. They can melt and boil very easily.
- Many non-metals are gases at room temperature.

Non-metals are Poor Conductors of Heat and Electricity

- Most non-metals are **insulators**.
- Electric charge cannot easily pass through them.
- Heat energy also cannot travel through a non-metal very easily.

> Graphite is a non-metal (a form of carbon) which can conduct electricity. Its atoms are arranged in layers with free electrons, which allow it to conduct electricity.

Non-metals are Brittle

- When solid, the forces between the particles are weak, which means they can break easily.
- Diamond (another form of carbon) is the exception here. It is very strong!

Non-metals are Dull

- Non-metals don't reflect light very well, which means they look dull.

✓ Check

1. Complete the table below with 'metal' or 'non-metal'.

Element property	Most likely to be a:
Shiny	metal
Brittle	
Electrical insulator	
Good conductor of heat	
Malleable	
Gas at room temperature	

2. Metals can be combined with other metals. What do we call the mixture? _____

3. Give **three** metals which are magnetic.

   _____ _____ _____

Endothermic and Exothermic Reactions

Recap

Signs that a chemical reaction has occurred include bubbling, a change in colour and a large change in temperature. Some chemical reactions release energy and get hotter but some can absorb energy and get colder.

Key Words
exothermic
endothermic
activation energy
catalyst

Revise

When a chemical reaction happens, energy is transferred to or from the surroundings. Typically, the energy transferred is heat energy so the reaction either feels hot or cold.

Exothermic Reactions

Chemical reactions which release energy to their surroundings are called **exothermic** reactions.

Combustion is a good example of an exothermic reaction. A burning fuel releases a lot of heat and light energy. Many oxidation and neutralisation reactions are also exothermic. Some exothermic reactions emit light energy instead of heat, such as the reaction inside glowsticks. Exothermic reactions can be used in hand warmers, or self-heating cans of food.

Glowsticks release light but the temperature does not increase.

> The reaction between a group 1 metal (such as sodium) and water is very exothermic!

Endothermic Reactions

Chemical reactions which take in energy from their surroundings are called **endothermic** reactions.

Endothermic reactions involve a drop in temperature, so they feel colder. Thermal decomposition is an example of an endothermic reaction. Mixing citric acid solution with bicarbonate of soda produces an endothermic reaction. We can use endothermic reactions in the cold packs that are used to treat sporting injuries.

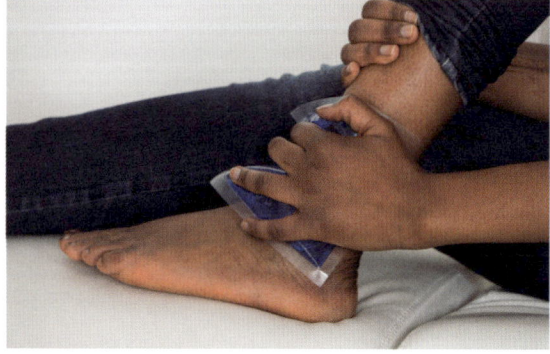

> To remember the difference, EXO sounds like Exit = Heat is leaving.

Respiration and Photosynthesis

- Respiration is an exothermic reaction. Heat energy is released.
- Photosynthesis is an endothermic reaction as light energy is absorbed by the chloroplasts.

Catalysts

A catalyst is a substance that speeds up a chemical reaction without being used up or chemically changed itself.

Chemical reactions take place only if a certain amount of energy is provided. This is called the **activation energy**. A **catalyst** is a substance that reduces the activation energy needed in a reaction, and so increases the rate of the reaction. Catalysts are useful because they can make chemical reactions happen more efficiently, which can save time and energy.

The catalyst is not used up in the reaction – it is not a reactant or a product. After the reaction it can be used again. In an equation, the name of the catalyst is written above the arrow.

A common catalyst is platinum. It is used in catalytic converters in car exhausts.

Manganese dioxide can be used to speed up the breakdown of hydrogen peroxide into water and oxygen.

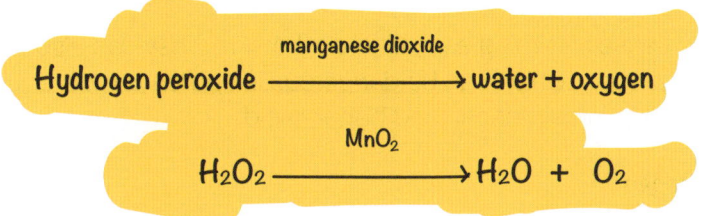

$$\text{Hydrogen peroxide} \xrightarrow{\text{manganese dioxide}} \text{water} + \text{oxygen}$$

$$H_2O_2 \xrightarrow{MnO_2} H_2O + O_2$$

Within our bodies, enzymes act as biological catalysts, speeding up many of the reactions that keep us alive. An example of an enzyme is amylase, which is found in our saliva. It breaks down starch into glucose.

✓ Check

1. Complete the paragraph below using the words in the box.

   > absorb   release   change   warmer   colder   harder

   Endothermic reactions _____ heat, while exothermic reactions _____ heat.

   This means that an endothermic reaction will make the surrounding area feel _____,

   while an exothermic reaction will make the surrounding area feel _____.

2. What effect does a catalyst have on the rate of a chemical reaction?
   _____

3. Are the following reactions endothermic or exothermic?

   a. Respiration _____

   b. Combustion _____

   c. Photosynthesis _____

   d. Thermal decomposition _____

Acids and Bases

Recap

Acids and **bases** are both chemicals that can be found in many different substances. They can be very useful but also need to be handled with care, as strong acids and bases can be quite dangerous.

Key Words
acid
base
pH scale
alkali
indicator
neutralisation
neutral

Revise

The pH Scale

Acids and bases can be measured on the **pH scale**, which ranges from 0 to 14. Acids have a pH value of less than 7, and bases have a pH value of more than 7. Chemicals with a pH of 7 are neutral.

Strong acids and bases are very dangerous and need to be handled carefully.

Acids

Acids taste sour and can often cause a burning sensation on the skin. They can also react with some metals to produce hydrogen gas, which can be dangerous if it builds up in a closed space. Some common acids include lemon juice, vinegar, and battery acid.

acid + metal ⟶ salt + hydrogen

Remember the test for hydrogen is a lighted splint. Burning hydrogen will make a loud 'pop'.

Alkalis/Bases

Many bases are insoluble, which means they do not dissolve in water. If a base does dissolve in water, we call it an **alkali**.

Bases taste bitter and can often feel slippery on the skin. They can also neutralize acids, which means that they can make an acid less acidic. Some common alkalis include baking soda, soap, and bleach.

Metals form oxides that are basic. Non-metals form oxides that are acidic.

Indicators

One way of seeing if a solution is acidic or alkaline is to use an **indicator**. An indicator is a coloured substance that changes colour at different pH levels. Indicators can be made using dyes from flowers, fruit and vegetables such as red cabbage. Red cabbage turns bright red in acid and blue in alkali.

- Indicator paper is paper soaked in indicator which makes it easy to use.

- Litmus paper comes in two forms, red or blue. Acids turn blue litmus paper red. Alkalis turn red litmus blue.
- Universal indicator paper is made from a mixture of different indicators. It can show a range of colours for different strengths of acidic and alkaline solutions.
- Using a datalogger to measure pH is much more accurate than using indicator paper.

Neutralisation

When an acid and a base are mixed together, they react. The base cancels out the acidity. The chemical reaction that takes place is called **neutralisation**. If they are mixed in the right amounts, the mixture will be **neutral** (pH 7). When an acid reacts with a base, it produces salt and water. Sometimes carbon dioxide is also produced.

Neutralisation reactions to remember:

acid + base → salt + water

acid + metal hydroxide → salt + water

acid + metal oxide → salt + water

acid + metal carbonate → salt + water + carbon dioxide

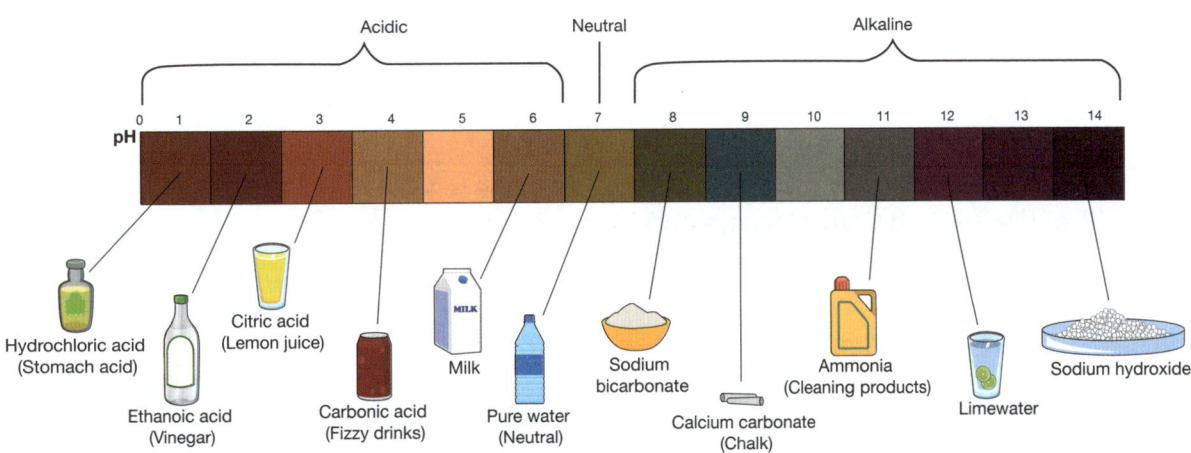

✓ Check

1. If you have too much acid in your stomach you might take an indigestion tablet (antacid).
   a. What type of chemical is an indigestion tablet made from? _____
   b. What is the name of the reaction between the tablet and an acid? _____

2. Complete these reactions:
   a. Nitric acid + sodium hydroxide → _____
   b. Hydrochloric acid + calcium carbonate → _____
   _____

3. Sulfuric acid has a pH of 1. What colour will it turn:
   a. Universal indicator paper? _____
   b. Blue litmus paper? _____
   c. Red cabbage indicator? _____

Metals and the Reactivity Series

↻ Recap

Some metals are more reactive than others. The metals in groups 1 and 2 of the periodic table get more reactive as you move down the groups.

Key Word
displacement

Revise

Reactivity Series

Some metals are very reactive, others are not very reactive and some are in-between.

The reactivity series is a list of metals with the most reactive at the top and the least reactive at the bottom.

By using the reactivity series, scientists can predict whether a chemical reaction will take place, and how reactive it will be.

Here are some of the major metals in the reactivity series, plus the non-metal carbon.

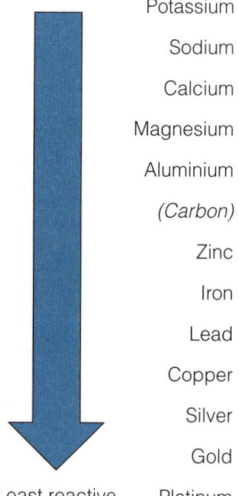

Very reactive
- Potassium
- Sodium
- Calcium
- Magnesium
- Aluminium
- (Carbon)
- Zinc
- Iron
- Lead
- Copper
- Silver
- Gold
- Platinum

Least reactive

Make up your own mnemonic to remember the order of the reactivity series. (e.g. Please Send Cats, Monkeys And (Crazy) Zebras…)

Displacement Reactions

If you mix a metal with a compound containing another metal, there's a chance of the metals swapping places.

The more reactive metal will displace the other metal and form a new compound.

If you mix zinc metal with copper oxide and heat it, the zinc will replace the copper and form zinc oxide.

zinc + copper oxide → zinc oxide + copper

The more reactive zinc has displaced the copper.

This is an example of a **displacement** reaction.

If you mix copper and zinc oxide nothing will happen because copper is less reactive than zinc.

Displacement Reactions in Solution

A more reactive metal will displace a less reactive metal in salt solutions too.

Putting zinc metal into copper sulfate solution (blue) will produce copper metal and zinc sulphate solution (clear).

zinc + copper sulfate → copper + zinc sulfate

Other displacement reactions:

> iron + copper sulfate → iron sulfate + copper
> magnesium + zinc sulfate → magnesium sulfate + zinc
> copper + iron sulfate → no reaction

Copper is less reactive than zinc, so it won't react.

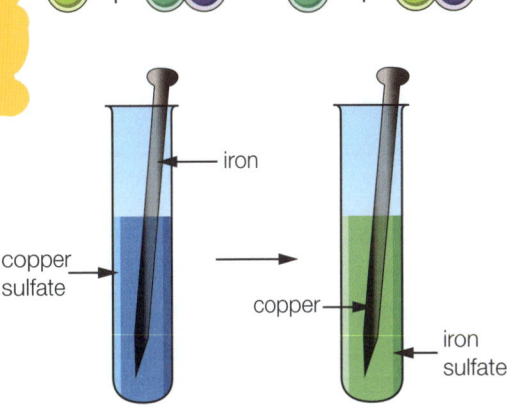

Reactions of Metals

A reminder of some of the reactions of metals you should know:

- Metals react with oxygen to form metal oxides.

> metals + oxygen → metal oxide

> potassium + oxygen → potassium oxide

- Metals react with water to produce a metal hydroxide plus hydrogen.

> metal + water → metal hydroxide + hydrogen

> sodium + water → sodium hydroxide + hydrogen

- Metals react with acids to produce a salt plus hydrogen.

> metal + acid → salt + hydrogen
> zinc + sulfuric acid → zinc sulfate + hydrogen

The position of the metal on the reactivity series will tell you how vigorous these reactions will be, or whether they will happen at all.

✔ Check

1. Would a reaction happen when:
    a. Zinc metal is added to magnesium sulfate solution? _____
    b. Iron metal is added to copper sulfate solution? _____
    c. Magnesium metal is added to iron sulfate solution? _____

2. Three metals are placed into test tubes of water. Metal X produces lots of bubbles, and a flame. Metal Y produces a few bubbles. Metal Z does nothing at all. Which of these metals do you think is:

    a. Silver? ____   b. Potassium? ____   c. Calcium? ____

3. Complete the sentence:

    The _____ reactive metal takes the place of a _____ reactive metal in a compound

    This is called a _____ reaction.

Metals and Ores

↻ Recap

Metals are usually found within rocks as **ores**. Over time we have become better at developing techniques to extract these metals from their ores.

Key Words
ore

📄 Revise

Metals low down in the reactivity series are found in the Earth as pure metals, such as gold. More reactive metals are found combined in compounds with other elements. These compounds are found as rocks called ores. It can be difficult to extract the metal from these ores.

For example: iron ore can be found as an ore called haematite which contains iron oxide. To extract the ore, we can heat the iron ore in a furnace with carbon and limestone.

It's thought that humans first discovered how to do this between 5000 and 3000 BCE, in Egypt. They heated iron ore with charcoal to get iron to use as tools and weapons. This was the start of the Iron Age.

carbon + iron(III) oxide → carbon dioxide + iron
$3C(s) + 2Fe_2O_3(s) \rightarrow 3CO_2(g) + 4Fe(l)$

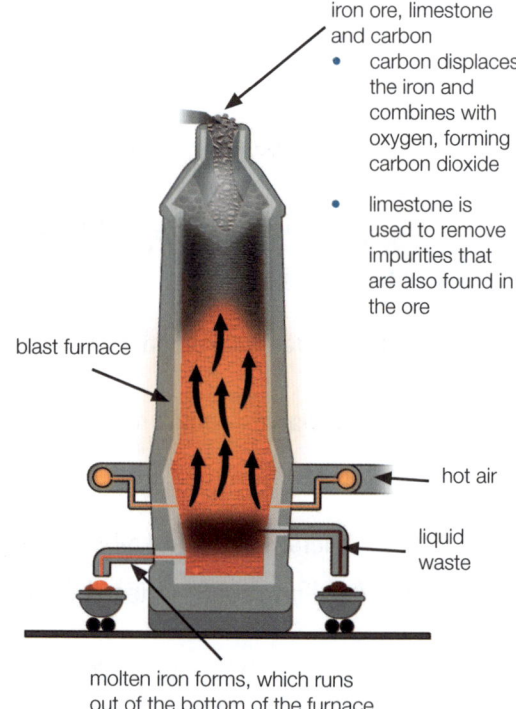

iron ore, limestone and carbon
- carbon displaces the iron and combines with oxygen, forming carbon dioxide
- limestone is used to remove impurities that are also found in the ore

blast furnace

hot air

liquid waste

molten iron forms, which runs out of the bottom of the furnace

Carbon can be used to extract any metal that is lower than it in the reactivity series. Such metals include iron, zinc and copper.

A chemical reaction where oxygen is removed from a compound is called reduction.

✓ Check

1. Which of these metals can you extract from their ore using carbon?

   aluminium, copper, zinc, magnesium

2. Complete the sentence:

   Carbon is able to displace the _____ in iron oxide because carbon is more _____.

3. Complete the word equation:

   carbon + iron oxide → _____ _____ + _____

Other Useful Materials

Recap

Different materials have different properties. The properties of a material make it useful for particular jobs. Some materials can be heated or joined together with other materials to produce new substances with different properties from before.

Key Words
ceramic
polymer
monomer
composite

Revise

Ceramics

Ceramic materials, such as glass, bricks and china, are made from heating soft substances such as clay in a very hot oven or kiln.

Ceramics are strong, hard and rigid. They are also brittle and can break if dropped. They have high melting points. Ceramics are good insulators of heat and electricity. The discs that connect electrical cables to pylons are made from ceramic.

Polymers

All plastic materials are made from **polymers**. Polymers are long molecules, made by joining much smaller molecules (**monomers**) together in long chains. ('poly' means 'many'.)
For example, poly(ethene) is made by joining lots of ethene molecules.

Polymers are usually:

- Insulators
- Flexible
- Low density
- Easily moulded

Composites

A **composite** material is made from two or more materials joined together. Composites have properties of both materials. For example: concrete, fibreglass and carbon fibre.

Concrete is made from mixing cement with sand and small stones. This makes it very strong.

Check

1. What property of ceramics makes it a useful material for a mug for hot drinks? _____
2. The Romans used cement as a building material over 2000 years ago.
   a. What did they add to the cement to make concrete? _____ _____
   b. Why is concrete better than cement on its own? _____
3. What do we call the small units that make up a polymer? _____

The Earth and Rocks

Recap

The Earth's **crust** is made of solid rocks. Under the crust is molten rock called **magma**. Rocks can be formed from sediments and when magma (liquid rock) comes to the surface as **lava** and cools.

Key Words
crust
magma
lava
mantle

Revise

Structure of the Earth

Planet Earth is roughly spherical. It is made up of three main layers: the crust, the **mantle** and the core.

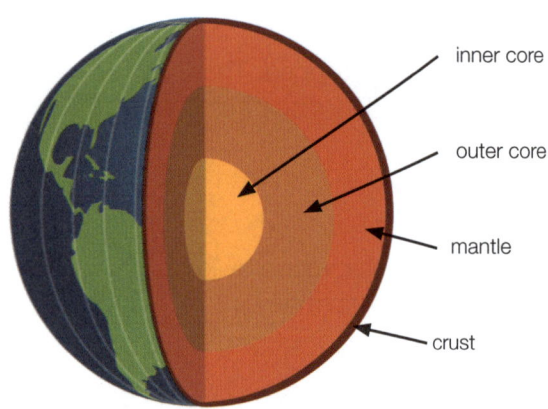

- Crust – Rocky outer layer (we live here!) made of interlocking tectonic plates which float around slowly on the mantle.
- Mantle – Semi-solid layer made from molten rock (magma). It moves very slowly, like a liquid.
- Core – At the centre of the Earth is a solid core, made of iron and nickel.

The Rock Cycle

There are three main types of rock and they change from one type to another over millions of years. This is called the rock cycle.

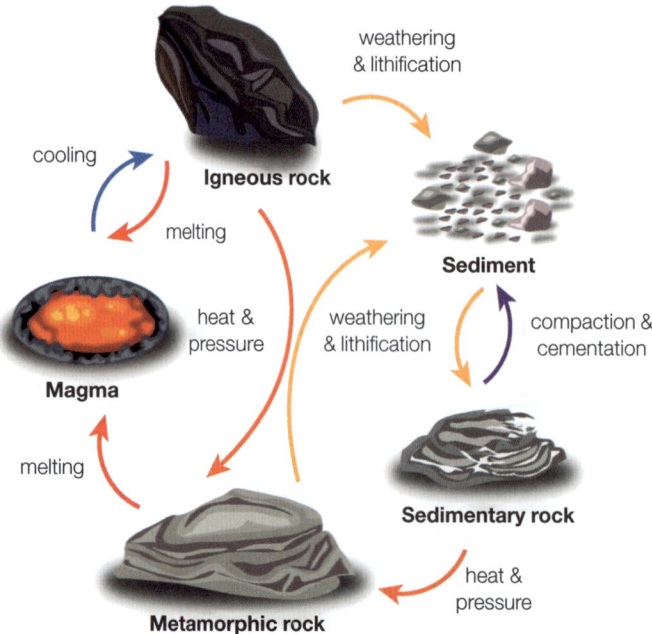

Igneous Rocks

Igneous rocks are formed from molten rock, called magma. Magma is sometimes forced out and erupts from a volcano. On the surface it cools to form igneous rocks. The quick cooling leads to small crystals, such as in basalt. Slow cooling leads to large crystals, such as in granite.

Magma and lava are basically the same thing. Below the crust it is called magma, and when it reaches the surface, it is called lava.

Sedimentary Rocks

Sedimentary rocks are formed from sediments. Sediments are made up of small grains of rock, and shells of dead organisms. These sediments build in layers over millions of years at the bottom of lakes or seas. Minerals dissolved in the water form crystals and cement the sediment together.

Sedimentary rocks often have fossils in them. Examples include limestone, sandstone and mudstone.

Metamorphic Rocks

Metamorphic rock is formed when existing rocks are changed by heat or high pressure. Rocks can become buried deeper in the earth or squeezed by tectonic plate movement. The heat and pressure cause chemical changes in the minerals within the rocks. Examples include slate, schist and marble.

Composition of the Crust

Rocks are made from different elements and compounds known as minerals. Common minerals include feldspar, quartz and calcite.

The crust of the Earth is mainly made from oxygen (47%) and silicon (28%). Other elements include aluminium (8%) iron (5%) and calcium (4%). These elements are usually found within oxides such as silicon dioxide, aluminium oxide, iron oxide and calcium oxide. These can combine with other elements and compounds to form different minerals.

✓ Check

1. Complete the table below for the types of igneous rock.

Size of crystals	Example rock type
large	
small	

2. Name the three layers of the Earth.

3. Which is the most common element in the Earth's crust? _____

4. Which type of rock is made:

   a. By magma/lava when it cools? _____

   b. From other rocks under heat or pressure? _____

   c. When grains of sediment build up? _____

Carbon and the Climate

🔄 Recap

Plants carry out photosynthesis which removes carbon dioxide from the air and converts it to sugar. Animals and plants use this sugar in respiration, which produces carbon dioxide gas.

Key Words
carbon cycle
photosynthesis
respiration
decomposers
fossil fuels
greenhouse gas
global warming
recycle

Revise

The Earth's Atmosphere

The Earth's atmosphere is made up of many different gases.

Oxygen is essential for all living things to stay alive.

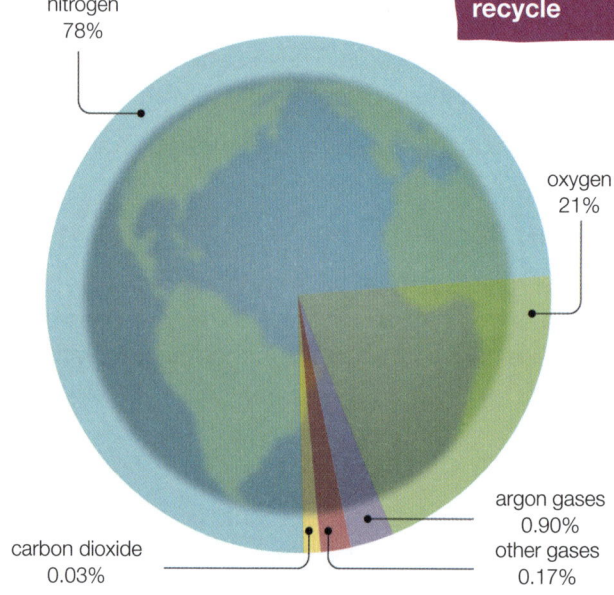

nitrogen 78%
oxygen 21%
argon gases 0.90%
other gases 0.17%
carbon dioxide 0.03%

The Carbon Cycle

The **carbon cycle** describes the continuous movement of carbon into and out of the atmosphere, animals, plants and the ground.

- Carbon exists in the atmosphere as carbon dioxide which is removed from the atmosphere by plants during **photosynthesis**.
- Animals eat plants, then release carbon dioxide by **respiration**. Plants release some carbon dioxide when they respire.
- Animal waste, and dead plants and animals are broken down by **decomposers**, releasing carbon dioxide back into the atmosphere.
- Some dead plants and animals become **fossil fuels** over millions of years. These are burned in power plants and vehicles which release carbon dioxide back into the atmosphere.

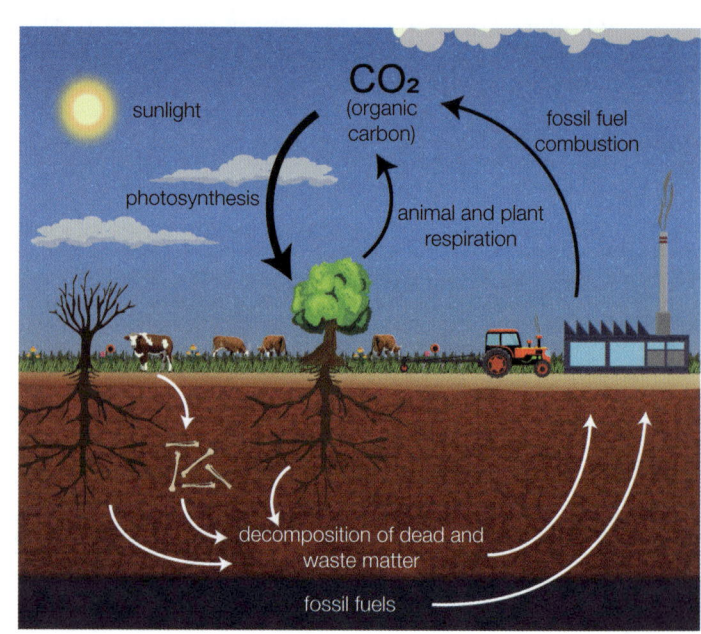

Human Impact on the Climate

For a long time, the amount of carbon in the atmosphere and in the Earth has been balanced. But, since the Industrial Revolution, human activity such as burning fossil fuels and deforestation has upset this balance. Carbon dioxide is being released far more quickly than is being removed, so the levels of carbon dioxide are increasing.

Carbon dioxide is a **greenhouse gas**. This means it traps the energy from the Sun, stopping it from escaping into space. This is warming up the Earth and its atmosphere. This temperature change is called **global warming** and this climate change affects atmospheric and ocean currents, causing much more extreme and unpredictable weather events, such as floods, hurricanes and droughts.

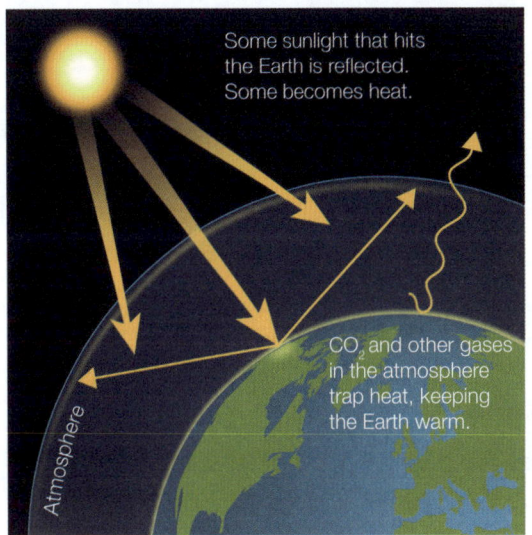

The greenhouse effect

Caring for the Environment

The Earth has a limited supply of resources. Fossil fuels such as coal, oil and gas took millions of years to form and they will eventually run out – they are not renewable energy resources. We also get raw materials from oil, such as lubricants and plastic polymers.

Metals in the Earth's crust need to be mined and extracted from their ores which uses a lot of energy, that mostly comes from burning fossil fuels. Mining also damages habitats.

Instead of throwing things away when we've used them, it's better for the environment if we reduce, reuse and **recycle** materials as much as we can. Doing this:

- Saves energy – new metals don't need to be extracted from ores. Fewer fossil fuels need to be extracted or burned
- Saves money – mining and extracting materials can be expensive
- Saves habitats as fewer mining and extraction sites are needed
- Reduces the amount of material going to landfill sites

✔ Check

1. a. Give **one** process that decreases the amount of carbon dioxide in the air.

   _____

   b. Give **two** processes that increase the amount of carbon dioxide in the air.

   _____   _____

2. Give **two** ways that humans have affected the levels of carbon dioxide in the last 100 years.

   _____   _____

3. Complete the sentences:

   Carbon dioxide is a _____ gas. It traps _____ from the Sun in the Earth's

   _____. This is causing global _____.

Forces

Recap

A force can be a push or a pull. The effect of forces can be seen everywhere. Forces can speed things up, slow things down, change their direction or change their shape.

Key Words
force
newtons
pivot
moment

Revise

Forces

Forces are pushes or pulls between two objects. You can't see a force, but you can see the effect it has on an object.

Forces can:

- Make a stationary object move
- Make a moving object stop, accelerate (speed up) or decelerate (slow down)
- Make a moving object change its direction
- Make an object twist or turn
- Change the shape of an object

Forces are measured in **newtons** (N) using a newton meter.

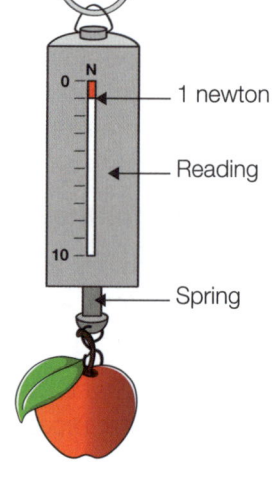

Force Diagrams

Force diagrams show the forces acting on an object. Forces are shown using force arrows. The arrow points in the direction of the force. The length of the arrow shows the size of the force.

In the diagram on the right, the two men are pushing in opposite directions. The forces are unbalanced.

- If the forces are acting in opposite directions, you subtract the forces to get the overall force.
- If they are acting in the same direction, you add them together to get the overall force.

In this example, the overall force can be calculated as 100 − 50 = 50 N

Balanced Forces

If the forces are the same size and acting in opposite directions, we say they are balanced.

When an object is not moving, it still has forces acting on it. The forces are balanced.

balanced forces = no change in movement
unbalanced forces = change in speed/direction

Moments

Forces can cause objects to rotate around a **pivot**. A pivot might be a spanner turning around a nut, your elbow or the centre of a seesaw. When a force acts on something with a pivot it creates a turning effect, called a **moment**.

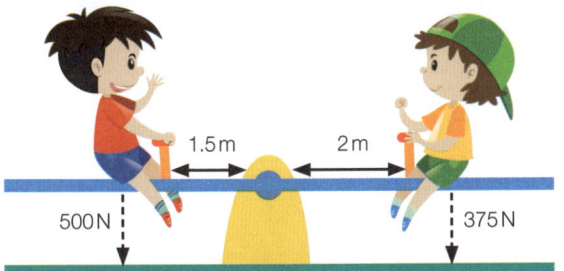

moment = force × perpendicular distance
(newton metres, Nm) (newtons, N) (metres, m)

The moments are the same, so the two children are balanced.

Moment on the left	Moment on the right
force × distance 500 N × 1.5 m =750 Nm	force × distance 375 N × 2 m =750 Nm

Measuring the Force Applied by a Muscle

You can measure the force a muscle applies to a bone. The arm is working as a lever, with the elbow as a pivot. It creates a moment.

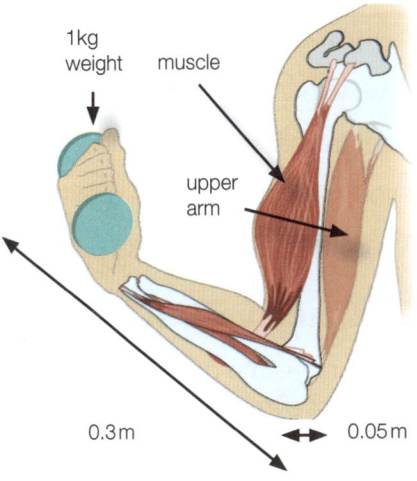

First, we need to calculate the moment:

- The 1 kg mass has a force of 10 N.

moment = force × perpendicular distance

- So, in the diagram, the moment of the mass is 10 × 0.3 = 3 Nm.

Then we work out the force applied by the biceps muscle:
- The muscle is applying a force to the arm to keep it still.

force = moment ÷ perpendicular distance

- We can rearrange the equation to calculate this force.

Force = 3 ÷ 0.05. So, the force being applied by the muscle is 60 N.

✔ Check

1. For each of these examples, say whether the forces are balanced or unbalanced:
   a. A car travelling at a steady speed on a motorway _____
   b. A motorbike speeding up when the lights turn green _____

2. In a tug of war, the red team pull to the left with a force of a 1000 N. The blue team pull to the right with a force of 800 N. What is the resultant force, and in which direction? _____
   _____

3. A force of 200 N is applied to the end of a seesaw, 3 m away from the pivot. Calculate the moment of the force. _____

Speed and Relative Motion

 Recap

Forces can make a stationary object move, and a moving object speed up, slow down or stop. A force can also change an object's direction of travel.

Key Words
speed
relative motion

Revise

Speed

Speed is a measure of how fast something is moving. To find the speed of an object you need to know two things: the distance it has travelled (in metres), and the time it takes to travel that distance (in seconds).

$$\text{speed (m/s)} = \frac{\text{distance travelled (m)}}{\text{time taken (s)}}$$

Speed is measured in metres per second, m/s. It is typically easier to measure the speed of things like vehicles in kilometres per hour, km/h.

For example, a sprinter ran 100 metres in 10 seconds.

speed = $\frac{100 \text{ metres}}{10 \text{ seconds}}$ speed = $\frac{100}{10}$ so, his speed = 10 m/s

Rearrange the Equation

If you know the speed and the time, you can calculate the distance

$$\text{distance} = \text{speed} \times \text{time}$$

A car travelling at 30 km/h for 2 hours will travel 30 × 2 = 60 km

If you know the distance and the speed, you can calculate the time

$$\text{time} = \frac{\text{distance}}{\text{speed}}$$

A car travelling 120 km for 3 hours will complete the journey in $\frac{120}{3}$ = 4 hours

Distance vs Time Graphs

A distance–time graph is a way of representing a journey. It shows you the distance travelled by an object over time.

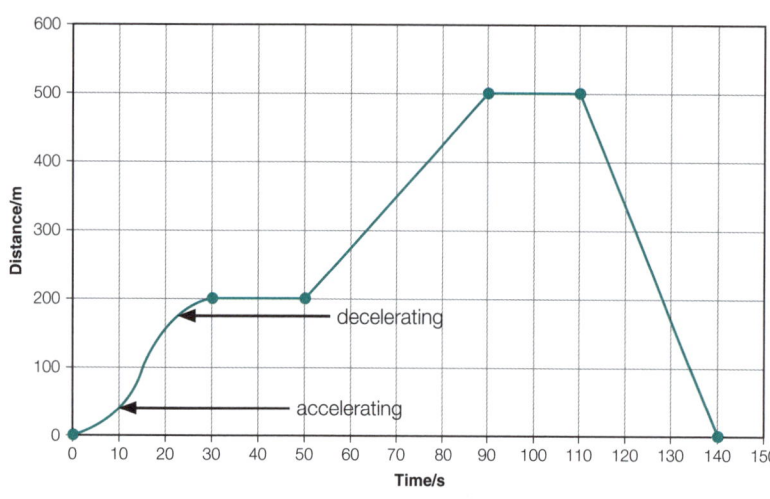

The line of the graph represents the speed of the object. A horizontal line means the object is stationary. The steeper the line, the faster it is travelling. You can calculate the speed at any point on the journey from the graph.

Between 50s and 90s the object travelled 300m: speed = $\frac{\text{distance}}{\text{time}} = \frac{300}{40} = 7.5$ m/s

Between 110s and 140s the object travelled 500m: speed = $\frac{\text{distance}}{\text{time}} = \frac{500}{30} = 16.67$ m/s

Relative Motion

The motion of an object is relative to an observer. If the observer is also moving, then this will change their view of how another object is moving. We call this **relative motion**.

Objects Moving in the Same Direction

A car travelling at 20 m/s moves past a car travelling at 10 m/s

Relative speed = 20 – 10 = 10 m/s

To a passenger in the slower car, the faster car is moving past at 10 m/s

> relative speed = fastest speed – slowest speed

Objects Moving in Opposite Directions

A car is travelling at 20 m/s. A second car is travelling in the opposite direction at 15 m/s

Relative speed = 20 + 15 = 35 m/s

To a passenger in one of the cars, it would seem like the other car is approaching at 35 m/s

> relative speed = speed of object 1 + speed of object 2

✓ Check

1. A car travels 50 km in 30 minutes. What is the average speed of the car in km/h?
   _____

2. What does the line on a distance–time graph tell you when it is:
   a. Horizontal? _____
   b. A straight line sloping upwards? _____
   c. A straight line sloping downwards? _____
   d. Curving upwards? _____

3. Train A is travelling at 50 m/s and train B is travelling at 40 m/s. To a passenger on one of the trains, what is their relative speed if they are:
   a. Travelling towards each other? _____
   b. Travelling in the same direction? _____

Friction and Drag

⟲ Recap

Falling objects experience **air resistance** as they move through the air. Parachutes have large surface areas to increase the air resistance and slow the parachutist down.

Key Words
air resistance
friction
drag

Revise

Friction

Friction is a force that occurs when things rub together. Friction always acts in the opposite direction to the movement.

Friction is helpful as it allows your shoes to grip the floor, tyres to grip a road surface and brakes on a bike to grip a wheel to slow movements down.

Friction can be unhelpful inside machines, as when surfaces rub parts they can wear down and get hot because of friction. This wastes energy as heat and means parts need replacing. Friction can be reduced by lubricating the surfaces.

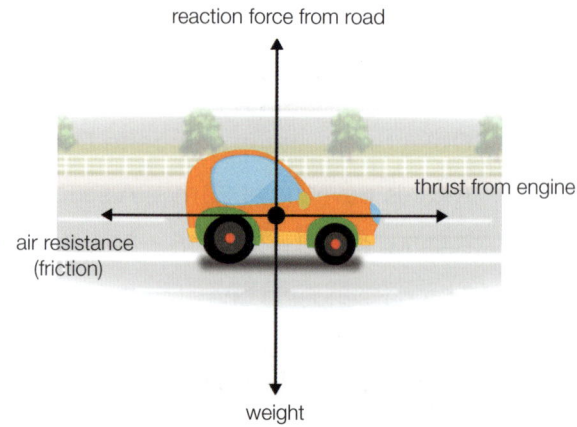

Rough surfaces: lots of friction
Smooth surfaces: less friction

Drag

Air makes friction with moving objects such as cars and planes. We call this air resistance or sometimes **drag**, because it slows the objects down. Parachutes have a large surface area to increase the air resistance and slow down a fall.

Objects moving through water experience water resistance. Objects that need to travel fast through air or water have a streamlined shape, which helps to reduce air or water resistance. Boats, fish and penguins are all streamlined.

✓ Check

1. Circle the correct word in each sentence:

   a. The greater the friction, the faster/slower an object will move.

   b. The lower the friction, the faster/slower an object will move.

2. What is the benefit of giving a car a streamlined shape?
   _____

3. On Earth, a feather falls much slower than a hammer. On the Moon, they fall at the same rate. Write a sentence to explain why.
   _____
   _____

Forces and Elasticity

Recap

As well as making objects move, forces can stretch and squash objects, changing their shape.

Key Words
equilibrium
joule

Revise

Stretching Forces

Forces can stretch or compress (deform) objects, such as a spring or an elastic band. Elastic materials can revert back to their original shape after being squashed or stretched. Inelastic materials will keep their new shape or break.

Hooke's Law

When a spring is stretched, the change in its length is called extension. If weights are added to a spring, there is a linear relationship between the size of the force and the stretch of the spring. Hooke's law says that the extension of a spring is directly proportional to the force applied to it.

This explains how newton meters work. We know the force applied due to the extension of the spring inside.

When the spring stops moving, the forces are balanced – they are in **equilibrium**. The weight downwards is the same as the force of the spring pulling upwards.

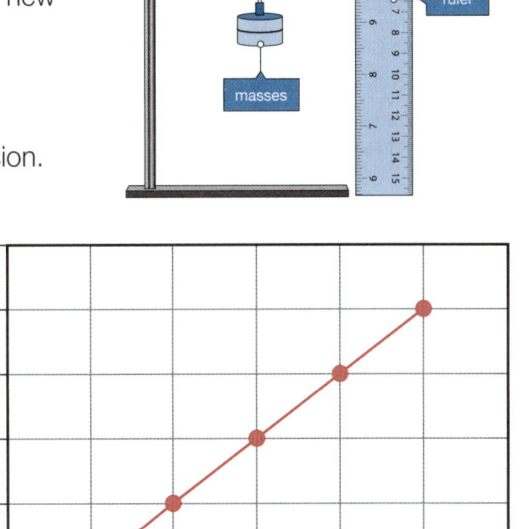

Work and Energy

We say 'work' is done if a force acts on an object and causes a change in that object. If an object is squashed or stretched, then work will have been done. Work is also done if an object speeds up, slows down or stops. Work is measured in newton metres, Nm or **joules**, J.

Check

1. Complete the sentence:

    Hooke's law says that the _____ of a spring is directly _____ to the _____ applied.

2. If a 1 N force causes a spring to extend by 2 cm, and a 2 N force causes the spring to extend by 4 cm, can you predict what the extension will be for:

    a. a 3 N force? _____
    b. a 5 N force? _____

3. What is the unit of work? _____

4. What word can we use when forces are balanced? _____

Pressure

Recap

The same size force acting over different sized areas will have different effects. A person in regular shoes might sink into soft snow but the same person wearing large snowshoes won't sink. Their weight is the same, but it is spread out over a larger area. We call this **pressure**.

Key Words
pressure
upthrust
density

Revise

Pressure

Pressure depends on the size of the force applied and the area it is applied to.

You can't press your thumb into a wall, but if you apply the same force to a drawing pin it will go into the wall. The head of the pin is much smaller, so the pressure is much higher. The unit of pressure is newtons per metre squared or N/m^2.

$$\text{pressure} = \frac{\text{force}}{\text{area}}$$

This block has a weight of 30 N. The area of each face is $4\,m^2$.

$$\text{pressure} = \frac{30\,N}{4\,m^2} = 7.5\,N/m^2$$

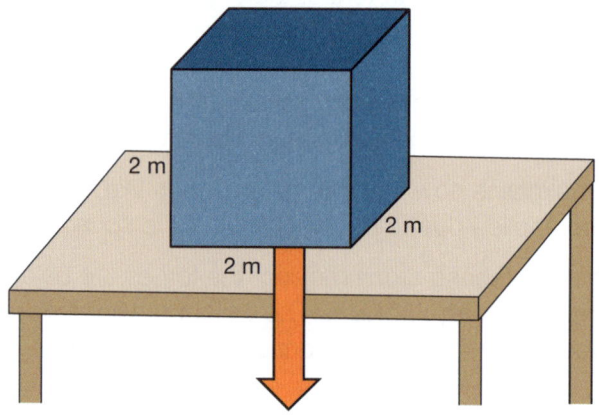

Pressure in Liquids

In a liquid, the pressure increases with depth. The deeper you go in a swimming pool, the more pressure you experience. This is because the weight of the water above you presses down on you, and the further down you dive, the more water there is above you.

Upthrust

When an object is put into water, the water pushes up on the object due to the amount of water being displaced. This upwards force is called **upthrust**.

If the upthrust is equal to the weight of the object, it floats. If the weight is greater than the upthrust, it sinks.

The **density** of the object is also important – a less dense material is more likely to float than a denser one.

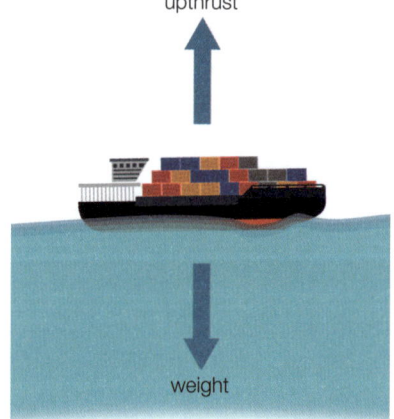

> The more salts that are dissolved in the water, the denser the water, and the greater the upthrust. This is why it's easier to float in very salty water, like in the Dead Sea.

Gas Pressure

A balloon contains gas under pressure. The pressure in a gas is caused by the gas particles colliding with the walls of the container. As they hit the sides, they exert a force.

Warming up the gas causes the particles to move faster. This means they collide more often with the walls of the container with greater force.

Making the volume of the container smaller will increase the number of collisions with the walls, increasing the pressure.

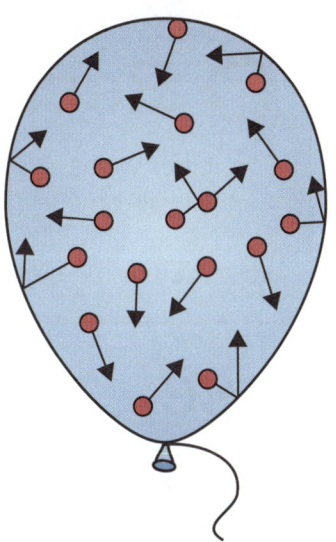

> **Warming** a gas → **increases** gas pressure
> Adding **more gas** to a container → **increases** gas pressure
> **Reducing** the **volume** of the container → **increases** gas pressure

Atmospheric Pressure

The weight of the atmosphere is constantly pushing down on us. We call this atmospheric pressure. At sea level the atmospheric pressure is the greatest as we have all of the atmosphere above us. As you travel higher up, there is less atmosphere above you pressing down, so the atmospheric pressure decreases.

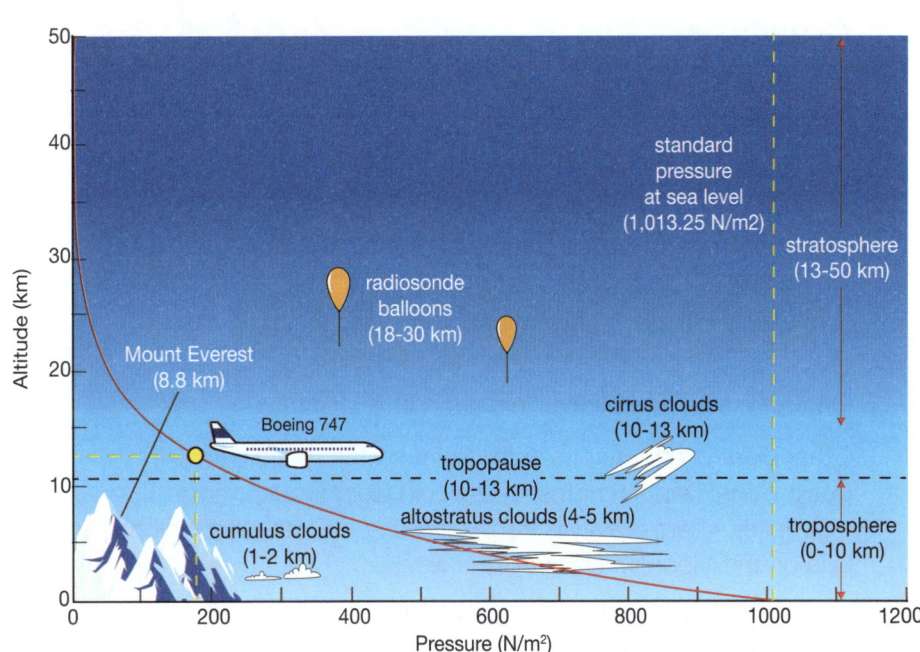

✓ Check

1. Complete the table below using your knowledge of the equation for pressure.

Force	30 N	68 N	50 N		20 N
Area	5 m²	2 m²	10 m²	4 m²	
Pressure				2 N/m²	0.5 N/m²

2. If an object weighing 800 N is floating in water, what is the upthrust? _____

3. Would a deep-sea diver experience a larger or smaller pressure than a scuba diver in shallow water? Explain your answer.

_____
_____

Non-contact Forces

Recap

The forces we have looked at so far work when one object is in contact with another. But some forces can act over a large distance, such as the gravitational pull of the Sun keeping all the planets in the solar system in orbit around it.

Key Words
gravity
weight
magnet
insulator
electric field
electric current

Revise

Non-contact Forces

Contact forces are applied when two objects touch.

Forces can also act over a distance. We call these non-contact forces. These include gravity, magnetism and static electricity.

Gravity

Gravity is a force which exists everywhere. It is a very weak force – something needs to have a very large mass (like a planet or star) before we notice its gravitational pull. Standing on the surface of the Earth, gravity pulls us towards the centre of the planet.

The **weight** of an object can be calculated as:

weight = mass × gravitational field strength (g)

On Earth, the gravitational field strength is 10 N/kg.

Other planets and moons in the solar system have different gravitational field strengths. You would weigh much more on Jupiter where gravity is stronger than on Earth, and weigh much less on the Moon where gravity is weaker.

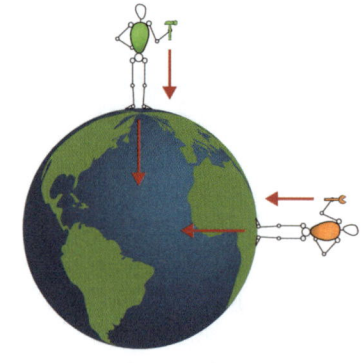

The pull of gravity gets weaker the farther you are from the centre of the mass. A person in an aeroplane would feel slightly less gravitational pull than a person standing on the ground.

Magnetism

Magnets produce a magnetic field around themselves. One end of the magnet is called the North (seeking) pole, the other end is the South (seeking) pole.

- If the poles are the same then they repel each other with a pushing force.
- If the poles are opposite then they attract each other with a pulling force.

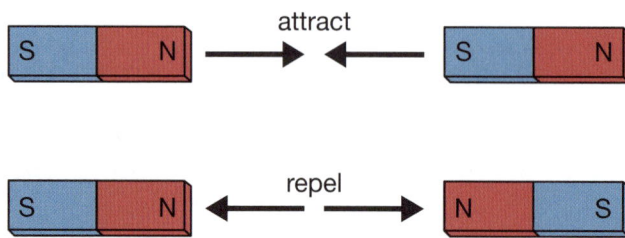

Static Electricity

There are two types of electrical charge: positive (+) and negative (-).

Most objects contain equal amounts of positive and negative charges and so are neutral. They are said to have no charge.

Negatively charged particles are known as electrons. Electrons can be transferred through friction by rubbing one insulator with another, such as rubbing a balloon with a jumper. Electrons move from one **insulator** to another.

The object that gains electrons becomes negatively charged.

The object that loses electrons becomes positively charged.

This imbalance of electric charges is known as static electricity.

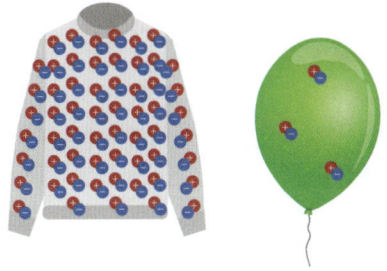

Before rubbing both the jumper and the balloon have an equal number of number of + and - charges

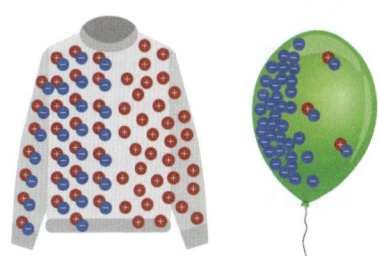

After rubbing the jumper has fewer - charges on it, the balloon has more - charges on it.

Electric Fields

A charged object creates an invisible **electric field** that surrounds it. The electric field can act across the space between objects even if they are not touching. Objects with the same charge will repel, and objects with opposite charges will attract.

You can also create an electric field by passing an **electric current** through a wire (see page 76).

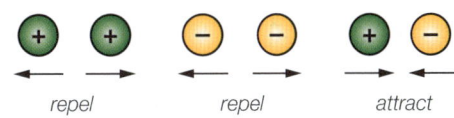

✔ Check

1. An object has a mass of 60 kg.

    a. What is the weight of the object on Earth? _____

    b. Will it weigh more or less on the Moon? _____

    c. Explain your answer to part b. _____

2. Will the following things attract or repel?

    a. A N pole and another N pole: _____

    b. A S Pole and a N pole: _____

    c. A positively charged object and a negatively charged object: _____

    d. Two negatively charged objects: _____

3. a. Forces that can act on objects without touching them are known as:
    _____

    b. Give **three** examples of these types of force:

    _____ _____ _____

Energy Stores and Energy Transfers

 **Recap**

Energy is all around us. It gives us the ability to do things. It gives us the ability to move, a lightbulb the ability to light up a room and an oven the ability to cook our dinner.

Key Words
law of conservation of energy
energy transfer
kinetic energy
chemical energy

 **Revise**

Storing Energy

Energy is the ability to do work. Energy is measured in joules (J).

There are eight types of energy store:

- Kinetic Store: The energy from any moving object, e.g. a runner or a car.
- Gravitational Store: The energy of a object at height, due to a gravitational field, e.g. an aeroplane or a book on a shelf.
- Chemical Store: The energy stored in chemical bonds such as those between molecules, e.g. fuels, food and batteries.
- Thermal Store: The total kinetic and potential energy of the vibrating particles in an object. The hotter an object is, the more energy it has stored, e.g. our bodies, hot stoves, etc.
- Elastic Store: The energy stored when an object is squashed or stretched, e.g. a rubber band or spring.
- Electric-Magnetic Store: The energy stored by magnetic objects in a magnetic field or charged objects in an electric field, e.g. a thundercloud or a fridge magnet.
- Vibration store: The energy stored in a wave moving up and down or a swing/pendulum moving back and forth, e.g. a clock pendulum.
- Nuclear Store: The energy stored in the nucleus of an atom, e.g. uranium and plutonium.

Energy Transfer

Energy cannot be created or destroyed, but it can be transferred from one energy store to another. This is called the **law of conservation of energy**.

Think about a rock falling off a cliff:

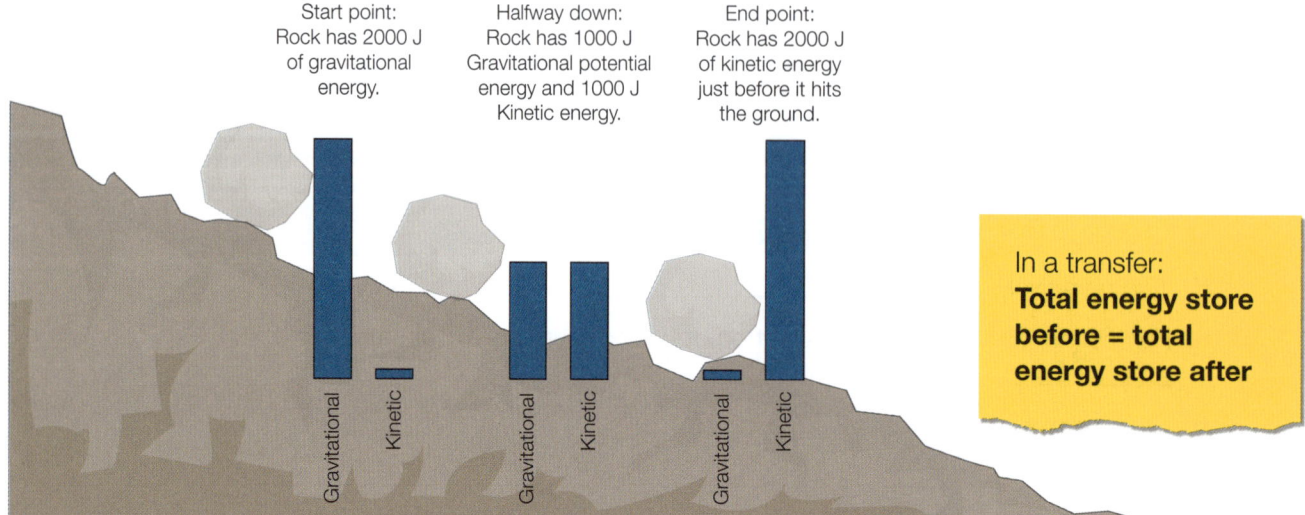

In a transfer:
Total energy store before = total energy store after

There are four main ways energy can be transferred between stores:

Mechanically – when a force is applied to move an object

Heating – when energy is transferred from hotter objects to colder objects

Electrically – when an electric charge flows

Radiation – when energy transfers as a wave, such as light or sound

Processes that involve **energy transfer**:

- Dropping an object: Dropping an object causes it to move through a gravitational field. Energy transfers from its gravitational energy store to its **kinetic energy** store.
- Stretching a spring: Releasing a stretched object, elastic energy is quickly transferred to a kinetic energy store.
- Completing an electrical circuit: **Chemical energy** in the battery is transferred to thermal energy in the filament of the bulb as well as some light energy.
- Burning fuels: Chemical energy store transferred to a thermal energy store. Some energy is transferred as light energy.
- Digesting and using food: Chemical energy stores in food can be used in many different ways by the body.

Energy Transfer Diagrams

We can represent these transfers as a transfer diagram.

An example for a book falling off a shelf is shown to the right.

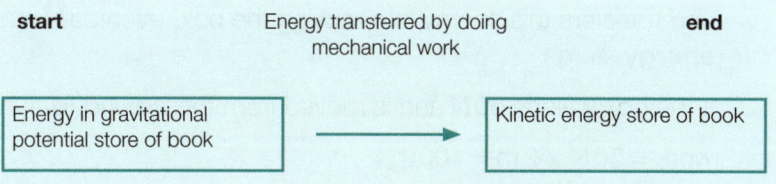

Dissipation of Energy

Not all the energy transferred becomes useful energy. Energy that has moved to a less useful store is dissipated. For example, a motor might waste energy through heating the surroundings and making sounds.

✔ Check

1. Complete the following sentence:

   Energy cannot be _____ or _____, it can only be _____ from one _____ to another.

2. What are the **four** ways energy can be transferred between stores?
   _____ _____ _____ _____

3. How is energy stored in the following objects?

   a. A moving train _____

   b. An apple hanging from a tree _____

   c. A bar of chocolate _____

   d. A stretched catapult _____

Work and Machines

🔄 Recap

Energy cannot be created or destroyed, but it can be transferred into other energy stores. When energy is transferred, we can calculate how much is transferred.

Key Words
gravitational potential energy
lever

📑 Revise

Energy Changes due to Forces

When a force moves an object through a distance, energy is transferred. We call the energy transferred the work done. To find out how much energy has been transferred we can use this equation:

work = force × distance
(joules) (newtons) (metres)

For example, a person lifting a box onto a high shelf needs a supply of energy (from their food) and transfers this energy into moving the box, eventually storing it in its **gravitational potential energy** store.

If the box weighs 50 N and is moved from the ground to a 2 m high shelf:

work = 50 N × 2 m = 100 J

Simple Machines

Simple machines such as **levers** allow us to change the amount of force needed to move something, but do the same work.

Levers make use of moments to act as a force multiplier. The size of a moment is affected by force and perpendicular distance. Levers make it easier to move heavy objects.

Gears and pulleys also work like this. They allow you to use a smaller force, but you need to move more.

The longer the distance between the pivot and the place where the force is supplied, the longer the perpendicular distance, and so less effort is needed to move the object.

✓ Check

1. What is the unit of energy? _____
2. What is the equation for calculating work done/energy transferred?
   _____
3. Calculate the work done in these situations:
   a. A person weighing 600 N moves 3 m up a flight of stairs. _____
   b. A cyclist pulls the brake levers with a force of 120 N, and travels 5 m before stopping.
      _____
   c. A ball weighing 100 N falls 10 m. _____

Transferring Thermal Energy

Key Words
thermal equilibrium
conduction
radiation
insulator

Recap

Matter is made of particles. When you heat up a material, the particles vibrate more, which means they have more kinetic energy. When you cool down a material, the particles vibrate less.

Revise

If there is a temperature difference between two objects, thermal energy (heat) will be transferred from the hotter object to the cooler object. This continues until they reach the same temperature. When no more heat is transferred, the two objects are said to be in **thermal equilibrium**.

Conduction

Heating an object, such as a metal rod, makes the particles inside it vibrate more. They gain energy in their kinetic energy stores. They bump into their neighbouring particles making them vibrate more. Kinetic energy is transferred from the hot end of the rod to the colder end, as shown in the diagram to the right. **Conduction** works best in solids where the particles are close together.

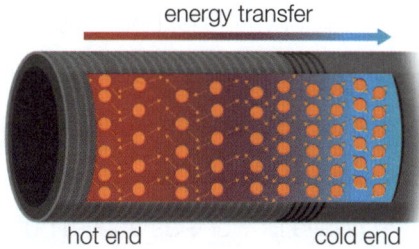

Radiation

Thermal energy can also be transferred without using particles. All objects radiate invisible waves of infra-red radiation. The hotter an object, the more energy it radiates. The cooler object absorbs the **radiation**. Because no particles are involved, the objects do not need to be touching.

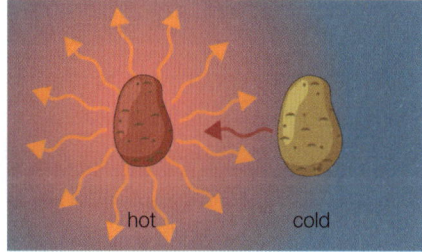

Insulators

Unlike conductors, **insulators** transfer thermal energy very slowly. Wrapping an object in an insulator slows down the rate at which energy is transferred to and from surrounding objects. Insulation can stop a hot object losing heat but also a cold object gaining heat.

Check

1. How is the heat being transferred in the following situations?

    a. A metal spoon put into a hot drink makes the handle hot. _____

    b. A hot cake on a cooling rack. _____

2. Complete the following sentence:

    Thermal energy moves from a _____ object to a _____ one.

3. What do we call it when two objects reach the same temperature? _____

4. Give an example of a material that is a:

    a. Good conductor _____   b. Good insulator _____

Fuels and Energy Resources

 **Recap**

Energy is stored in many different ways. This energy can be transferred to our homes and used in different ways by the appliances in our homes.

Key Words
biomass
non-renewable
renewable
power rating

 **Revise**

Energy from the Sun

The Sun is the ultimate source of most of our energy resources:

- Food – plants transfer energy from the Sun into chemical energy stores through photosynthesis. Energy is transferred again when the plants are eaten by people or animals.
- **Biomass** – as above, but energy is transferred when plants are burned.
- Fossil Fuels – as above, but plants die and are fossilised over millions of years.
- Wind Power – Sun's energy heats the atmosphere and makes the air circulate, causing winds.
- Wave Power – as above, but the winds make the water move as waves.
- Solar Power – solar cells can transfer the energy from the sun into electricity.

Note: Nuclear power and geothermal power do not come from the Sun.

A fuel stores energy in its chemical energy stores. It transfers this energy when it burns, e.g. biomass and fossil fuels.

Fossil fuels take millions of years to form. We call these **non-renewable** as no more will be made. Energy sources that do not run out are called **renewable**.

Electricity in the home

Electrical appliances in the home transfer energy via electrical work into other energy stores such as kinetic, radiation and thermal energy.

All appliances have a **power rating**. Power is the amount of energy transferred each second by the appliance.

Power is measured in watts (W) or kilowatts (kW). 1 watt = 1 joule transferred per second.

power = voltage × current
p = V × I

The energy transferred by an appliance can be calculated with this equation:

energy transferred (in kWh) = power (kW) × time (h)

The energy transferred is measured in kilowatt hours (kWh).

A 4 kW heater turned on for 3 hours uses:

4 kW × 3 h = 12 kWh

The symbol for current is I, from the French phrase intensité du courant (current intensity).

Energy Bills

Energy companies monitor how much energy is transferred to our homes using meters. They calculate how many kWh of energy, or "units", a household has used, then charge a set amount per unit.

For example, if electricity costs 16p per kWh, a heater using 12 kWh would cost £0.16 × 12 = £1.92 to run.

Electricity	
Total kWh used	1143
Cost	
1143 at 2.9p per kWh	£33.15
Total cost of electricity used	**£33.15**

Gas	
Total kWh used	1579
Cost	
1579 at 17.1p per kWh	£270.01
Total cost of gas used	£270.01
Electricity and Gas Total	**£303.16**

Energy in Foods

The three chemicals that act as energy stores in food are carbohydrates, fats and protein. Carbohydrates (sugars) and fats contain the most energy.

Food labels tell you how much energy is in each food. Energy in food is measured in kilocalories (kCal) or kilojoules (kJ).

Nutrition				
Typical values	100 g contains	Each slice (typically 44 g) contains	% RI*	RI* for an average adult
Energy	985 kJ / 235 kCal	435 kJ / 105 kCal	5%	8400 kJ / 2000 kCal
Fat	1.5 g	0.7 g	1%	70 g
of which saturates	0.3 g	0.1 g	1%	20 g
Carbohydrate	45.5 g	20.0 g		
of which sugars	3.8 g	1.7 g	2%	90 g
Fibre	2.8 g	1.2 g		
Protein	7.7 g	3.4 g		
Salt	1.0 g	0.4 g	7%	6 g
*Reference intake of an average adult (8400 kJ/2000 kCal)				

✔ Check

1. Which **three** types of chemicals in food act as energy stores?
   _____ _____ _____

2. Give an example of a non-renewable energy source. _____

3. Give **three** examples of renewable energy sources.
   _____ _____ _____

4. A heater with a rating of 3 kW is switched on for 2 hours.
   a. How much energy has the heater transferred? _____
   b. If one kWh costs 15p, how much did it cost to run the heater? _____

Electrical Circuits

Recap

A battery is a chemical energy store. When it is connected to a circuit, electrical work is done, transferring energy each component in the circuit. Particles called electrons have a negative charge. These particles can move freely through conductors such as metals.

Key Words
ammeter
potential difference
voltmeter
resistance

Revise

Current

An electric current is the flow of charge (negative electrons) around a circuit. You need a complete circuit for electricity to flow. The rate of flow of charge is called the current which is measured in amperes (A) using an **ammeter**.

The battery acts like a pump; it provides energy to the electrons, pushing them around the circuit. The size of this pushing force is called the **potential difference** (p.d.). Potential difference is measured in volts (V) using a **voltmeter**.

Adding an additional battery will produce a bigger push, moving the charged particles more quickly. So, increasing the potential difference will increase the flow of current.

Series Circuits

In a series circuit the components are connected end to end, forming a single loop. There is only one path for the current. If a bulb breaks or a wire is removed, the circuit is broken and all the components stop working. Current is the same everywhere in the circuit.

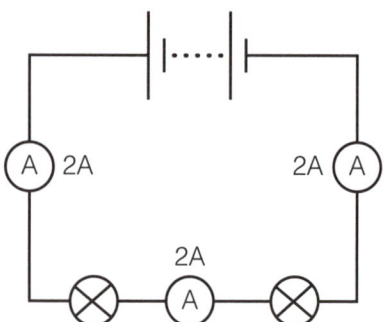

Important: current is not 'used up' as it moves through the circuit.

The potential difference across the components adds up to the potential difference of the cell/battery.

Total cell p.d. $V_s = V_1 + V_2 + V_3$

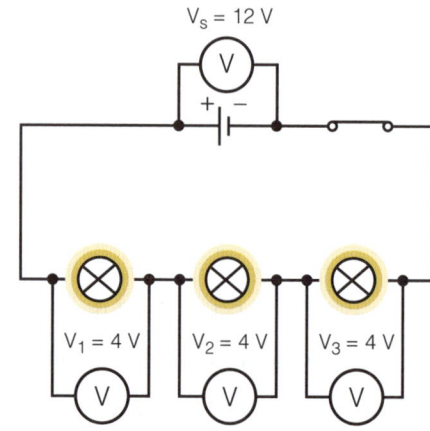

Parallel Circuits

Parallel circuits have several loops. In a parallel circuit, if a lamp breaks or a component is disconnected, the other components continue working. This is because current continues to flow along the other paths in the circuit. The current is shared between the different loops, then meets up again. Switches can turn individual components on and off, like the lights in our homes.

The potential difference across each bulb is the same as the potential difference of the cell. Potential difference is not shared. $V_1 = V_2 = V_3$

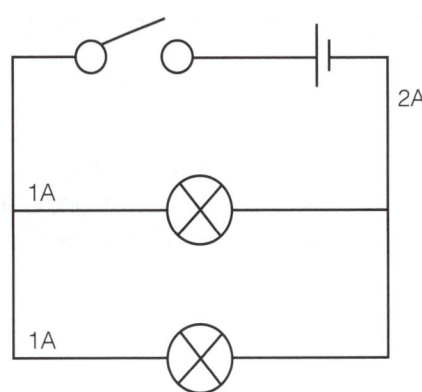

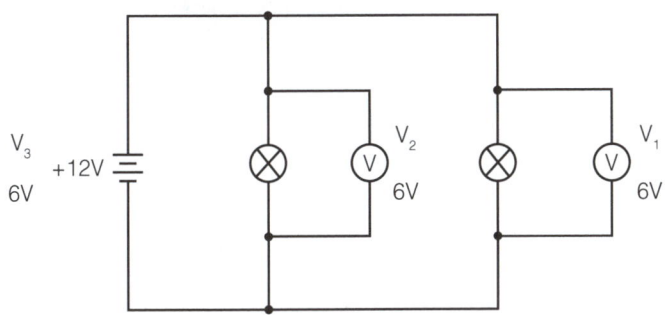

Resistance

Resistance is a measure of how easily current can flow through a component. It is measured in ohms (Ω).

- Conductors have low resistance. Charge can flow easily.

- Insulators have high resistance. Charge cannot flow.

Resistance can be calculated using this formula:

$$R \text{ (Resistance } (\Omega)) = \frac{V}{I} = \frac{\text{potential difference (V)}}{\text{current (A)}}$$

Common Circuit Symbols

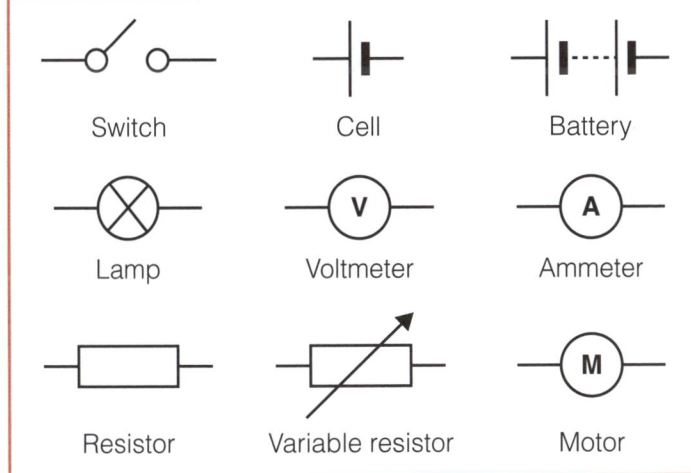

✓ Check

1. Current is the flow of what? _____

2. What is the force that pushes current around a circuit? _____

3. With what units do we measure resistance? _____

4. What does an ammeter measure? _____

5. The current in a circuit is 2 A. The potential difference across a component is 0.2 V. What is the resistance of the component? _____

Magnets and Electromagnets

Recap

Magnetism is a non-contact force. Magnets are surrounded by a magnetic field. If two magnets are brought together, two like poles will repel each other and two unlike poles will attract.

Key Words
alloy
magnetic field
electromagnet

Revise

Magnets

Permanent magnets are made of metals such as iron, cobalt and nickel and their **alloys**.

When allowed to hang freely, one end of a magnet points north, and we call this the north pole of the magnet. Not surprisingly, the other end of the magnet (the south pole) points south!

The magnet is surrounded by invisible **magnetic field** lines. Field lines run from the north pole of the magnet to the south pole. They can be 'seen' using a plotting compass or sprinkling iron filings onto paper, as shown in the diagram to the top right.

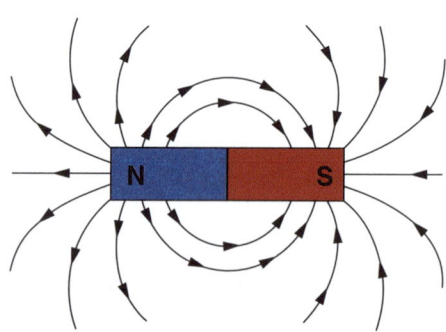

The closer the field lines are, the stronger the magnetic field.

Earth's Magnetic Field

The centre of the Earth is made from iron and nickel. This makes the Earth act like a bar magnet. We can use a compass to navigate because it points to the Earth's magnetic north pole. The magnetic north pole is not in the same position as the true geographic north pole – and it drifts around by about 55 kilometres a year.

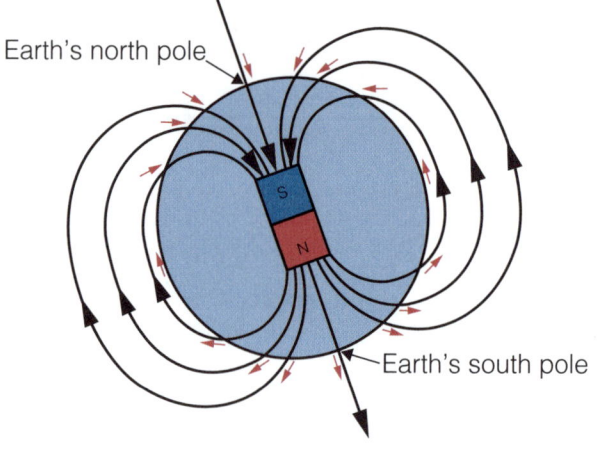

Electromagnets

A temporary magnet can be made by passing an electric current through a wire. The magnetic field lines are circular around the wire and are weak. The lines are closer together nearer the wire where the field is stronger.

Electromagnets can be made stronger by:
- Coiling the wire
- Increasing the current
- Using a core from a magnetic material such as iron

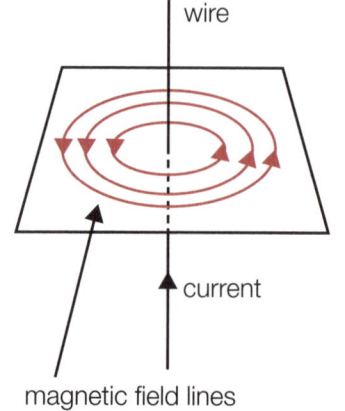

Switching off the current turns off the magnetic field. Electromagnets are useful in scrapyard cranes, electric bells, loudspeakers and automatic door locks.

DC Motors

Electromagnets are also very useful in motors. A motor uses an electromagnet between the poles of permanent magnets.

When a DC current is passed through the wire in a magnetic field it will cause the wire to move. This is called the motor effect.

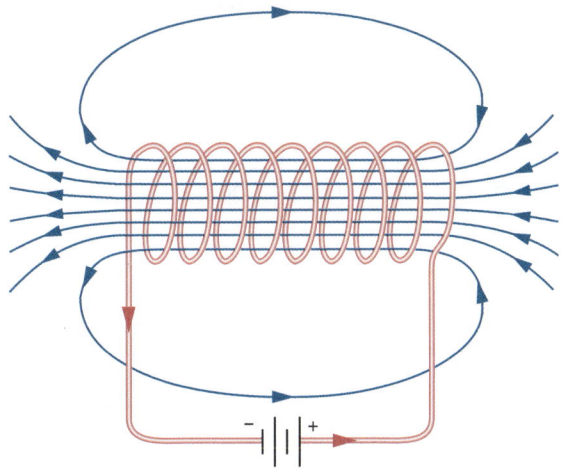

Magnetic field lines around a coil of wire or solenoid.

To increase the speed of the motor:

- Increase the current
- Use stronger magnets (increase magnetic field strength)

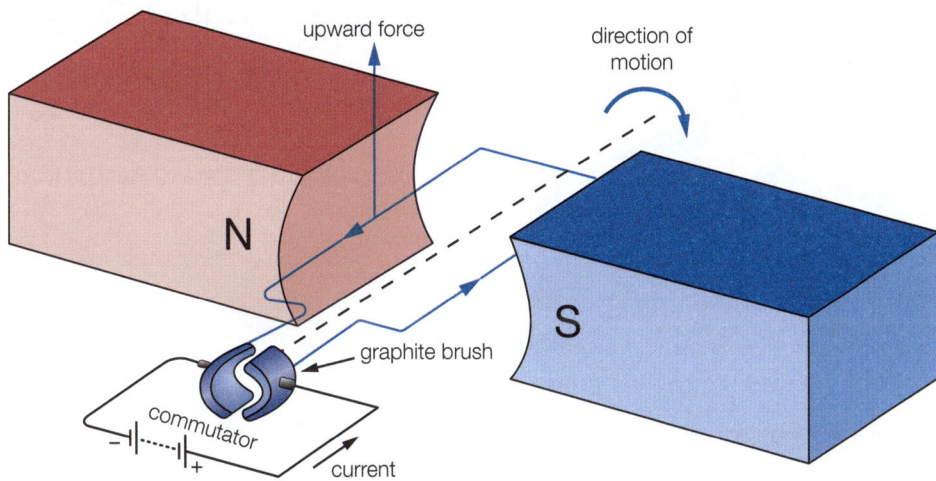

✔ Check

1. Give **three** ways you can make an electromagnet stronger.
   _____ _____
   _____

2. Give **two** ways you can increase the speed of an electromagnetic motor.
   _____ _____

3. Which of these metals would make a good core for an electromagnet:
   iron, copper, gold or nickel? _____

Properties of Waves

Recap

Light and sound are two examples of **waves** you will have already heard about. Waves transfer energy from one place to another.

Key Words
wave
transverse
amplitude
peak (crest)
trough
wavelength
frequency
superposition

Revise

Observing Waves in a Ripple Tank

You can observe waves in water using a ripple tank. Vibrations cause the water to move up and down, making waves. Water waves are **transverse** waves – the direction of travel is at right angles to the up and down undulations of the wave. Light also travels as a transverse wave.

Each part of the wave moves up and down only. A boat with its engine not running would move up and down and remain in the same spot.

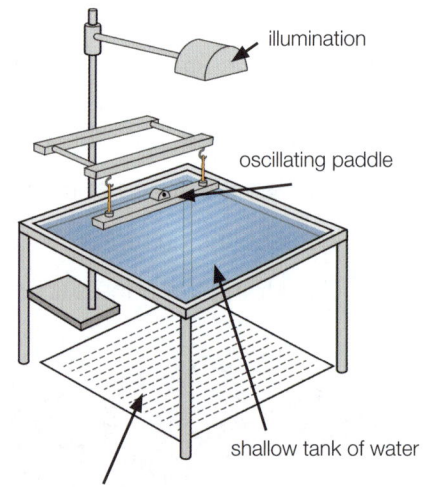

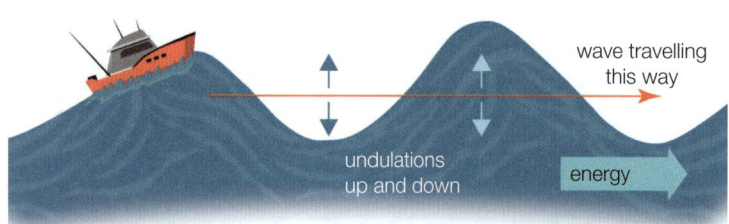

Features of a Wave

- The **amplitude** is the height of the wave from the centre.
- The highest part of a wave is the **peak** (or **crest**).
- The lowest part of the wave is the **trough**.
- The distance from a point on one wave to the corresponding point on the next wave is the **wavelength**.
- **Frequency** is how many waves pass by a given point in one second. Waves that are close together have a high frequency. Waves that are spread out have a low frequency. Frequency is measured in Hertz (Hz).

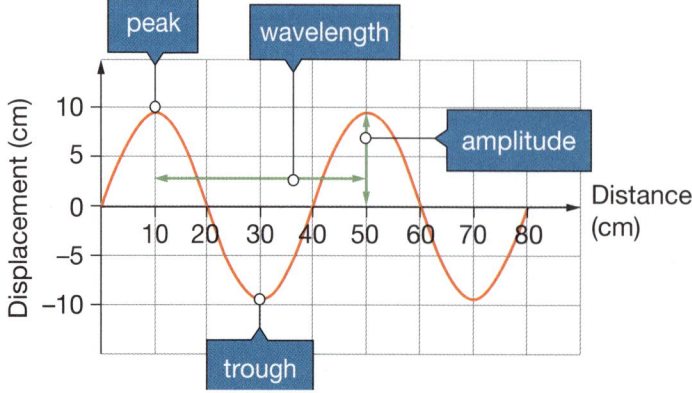

Reflection of Water Waves

If water waves hit a surface they will be reflected. The direction of the wave changes. The waves reflect at the same angle as they hit the wall. (angle *i* = angle *r*)

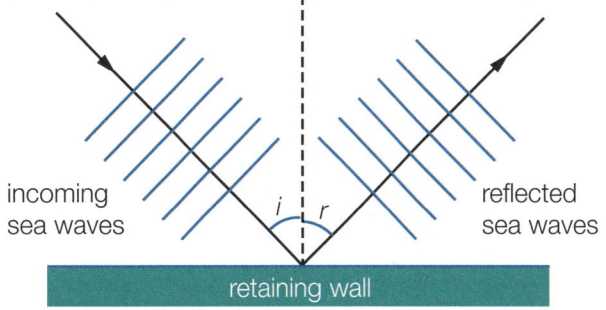

Superposition

If two water waves meet, they can combine briefly. This is called **superposition**.

- If two peaks meet, they add together and the wave gets bigger.
- If two troughs meet, they add together and get deeper.
- If a peak meets a trough they cancel each other out.

Superposition is also called interference.

Light Waves vs Sound Waves

Sound waves must have a medium to travel through (e.g. air particles).

Light waves do not need a medium and can travel through a vacuum.

Light waves travel much faster than sound waves:

- Speed of light in a vacuum = 300 000 km/s
- Speed of sound in air = 340 m/s

Sound travels faster in a liquid or a solid, as the particles are closer.

✔ Check

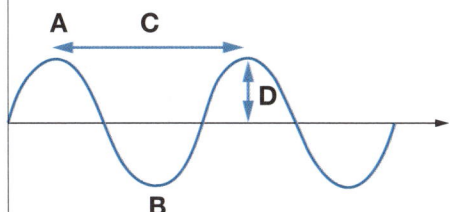

1. Label the parts of the wave to the right.

   A _____ B _____

   C _____ D _____

2. Briefly say what happens to the two waves if:

   a. A peak of one wave meets the peak of another wave

   _____

   b. The trough of one wave meets the trough of another wave

   _____

   c. The peak of one wave meets the trough of another wave.

   _____

2. What device can we use to observe waves in water? _____
3. Which waves are faster – sound or light? _____

Light Waves

Recap

Light is an example of a transverse wave. Light does not need a medium to travel through; it can even travel through the vacuum of space. Light travels incredibly fast; the speed of light in a vacuum is 300 000 km/s.

Key Words
reflection
law of reflection
refraction
convex lens

Revise

Light and Materials

When light hits the surface of an object the light might be absorbed or reflected. If the surface is rough, light is scattered in different directions. If the surface is smooth, like a mirror, light is **reflected** in a single direction.

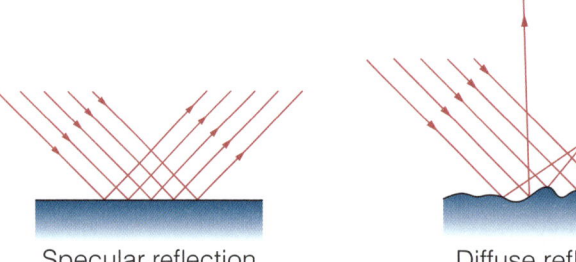

Specular reflection   Diffuse reflection

Law of Reflection

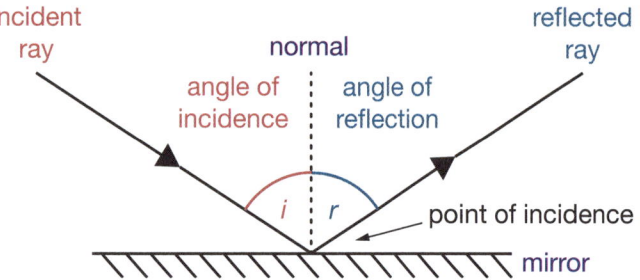

When light hits the surface of a plane mirror, it reflects. We can show this with a ray diagram.

The **law of reflection** states that:

the angle of incidence (i) = the angle of reflection (r)

Refraction

Refraction is when light bends when it crosses a boundary – such as air into water or air into glass.

When light goes from a less dense medium to a more dense medium it will bend towards the normal. When light goes from a more dense medium to a less dense medium it will bend away from the normal.

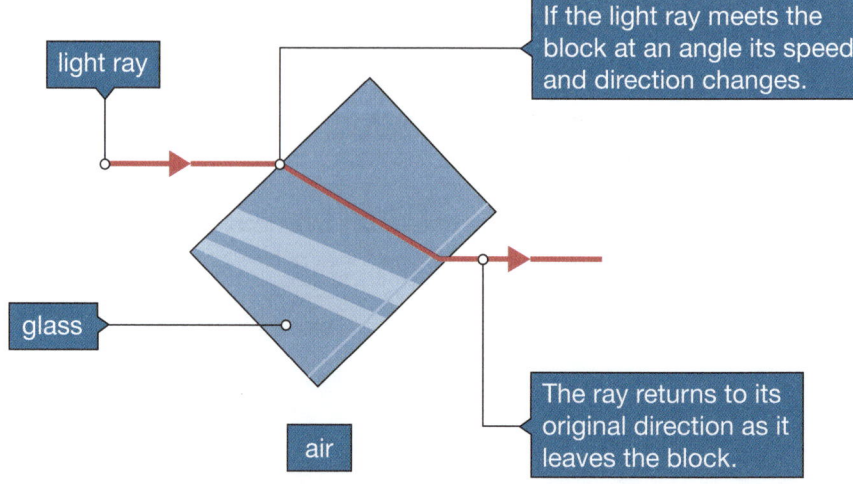

If the light ray meets the block at an angle its speed and direction changes.

The ray returns to its original direction as it leaves the block.

Pinhole Camera

The pinhole camera is a very simple device which can be made using just a light-proof box and photographic film. Light passes through a small hole made in the front of the box. The image on the film is upside down.

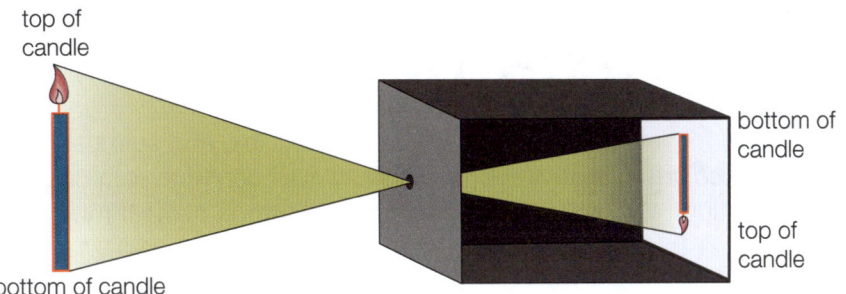

How the Eye Works

The eye is very similar to a pinhole camera. The image on the retina at the back of the eye is upside down. The eye uses a **convex lens** to focus the image onto the retina. Lenses bend light through refraction.

The iris is the coloured part of the eye. It controls the amount of light entering the eye by changing the size of the hole (the pupil) in the eye.

Special cells in the retina are photo-sensitive. When hit by light they send a signal to the brain.

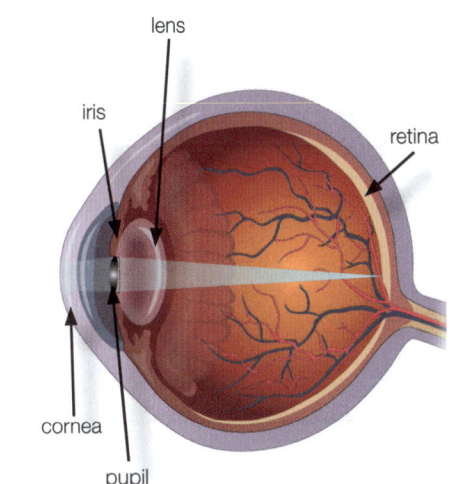

Light and Colour

Visible light is known as white light and is made up of many colours of light. White light can be split by a prism. Each colour has a different frequency. This is the visible spectrum.

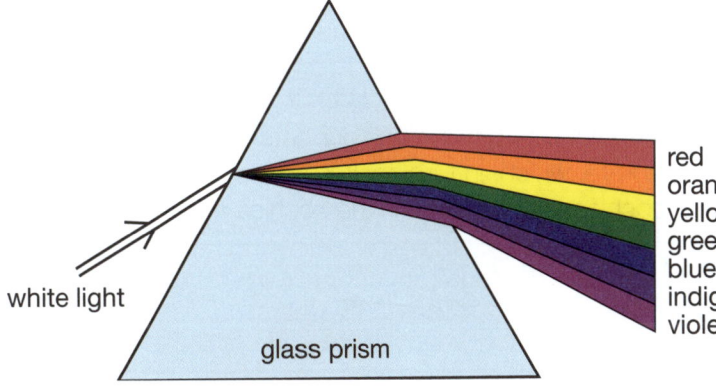

Check

1. What is the role of the lens in your eye?
   _____

2. What is the law of reflection?
   _____

3. Complete these sentences:
   a. When light goes from a less dense medium to a _____ medium it bends _____ the normal.
   b. When light goes from a more dense medium to a _____ medium it bends _____ from the normal.
   c. When light bends, we call it _____.

Sound Waves

Recap

Sound waves travel as a vibration of particles, and so must have a medium to travel through. Sound waves can't travel through a vacuum. We hear sounds because **vibrations** travel through the air to our ears.

Key Words
vibrations
longitudinal
pitch
echo
ultrasound

Revise

How Sound Travels

Sound waves are **longitudinal** waves, which means that the particles vibrate in the direction of travel.

Sound is produced when an object vibrates. Pressure waves transfer energy from one place to another.

The speed of sound is affected by how close the particles are. Sound is fastest in a solid and slowest in air. Sound is faster in warmer air or liquid than colder air or liquid.

Speed of sound in:

- air = 340 m/s
- water = 1500 m/s
- wood = 4000 m/s

How We Hear

Vibrations in the air reach our ears and travel down the ear canal. This makes your eardrum vibrate, which, in turn, makes your ear bones vibrate. These bones transmit vibrations to the cochlea. Hairs vibrate in the cochlea and send a message to the brain.

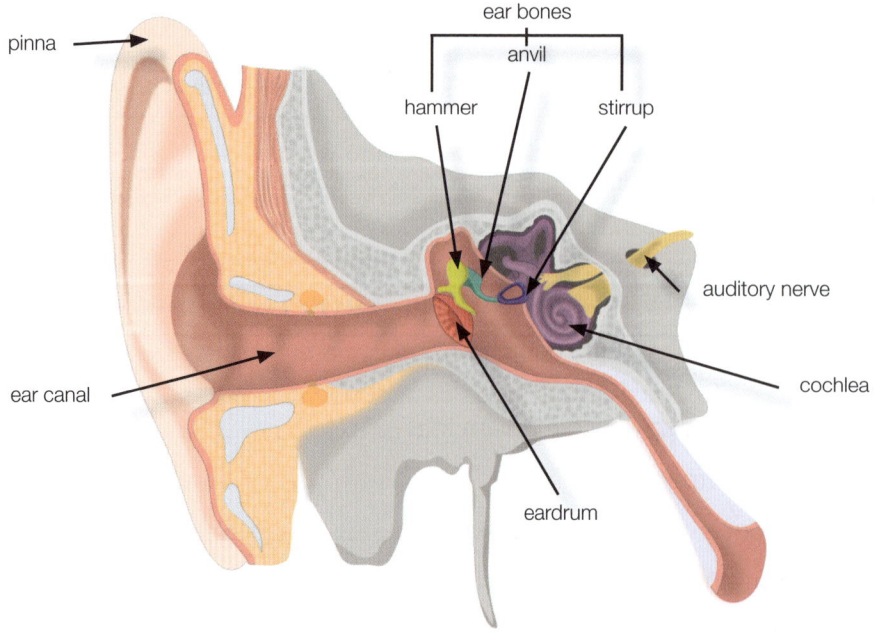

Frequency of Sound

The frequency of sound is how many waves pass by in one second. Frequency affects the **pitch** of the sound. A high frequency sound is high pitched and low frequency sounds are low pitched.

Frequency is measured in Hertz (Hz). The auditory range of:

- humans is typically 20 to 20 000 Hz
- dogs is typically 40 to 60 000 Hz
- bats is typically 9000 to 200 000 Hz!

Echoes and Absorption

Sound can be reflected just like light when it hits a hard surface. Reflected sound is called an **echo**. Soft objects such as carpets and curtains absorb sound and can reduce echoes.

Recording studios use special acoustic panels to improve sound quality. They are made of sound-absorbing materials and specially shaped to reduce echoes and unwanted noise.

Ultrasound

Humans cannot hear sounds above 20 000 Hz; sounds above this threshold are called **ultrasound**. Ultrasound can be used to clean objects such as jewellery and can also be used in medicine. Ultrasound scans can be used to make images of a developing fetus inside the womb or to view soft organs inside the body.

Microphones and Speakers

A microphone converts a sound wave into an electrical signal.

Inside a microphone, sound waves hit a membrane attached to magnets. The motion of the magnets causes a changing electrical signal that can be recorded.

A loudspeaker is a microphone in reverse. Electrical signals change the strength of an electromagnet which moves magnets attached to a membrane. This causes vibrations which we can then hear.

✓ Check

1. Through which medium does sound move:
    a. The fastest? _____
    b. The slowest? _____
2. What medium can sound not travel through? _____
3. If you increase the frequency of a sound, what happens to the pitch?
   _____

Earth and Space

Recap

You already know that massive objects like stars and planets have gravitational pulls large enough to be measured. The gravitational pull of something as large as our Sun is strong enough to keep even the most distant planets in our solar system in orbit around it.

Key Words
star
galaxy
light year

Revise

Day Length and Seasons

The Earth is tilted slightly on its axis. This tilt is the reason for our seasons.

When it is summer for the Northern Hemisphere – the north is tilted towards the Sun. The radiation from the Sun is more direct, and more concentrated, which leads to the warmer summer temperatures.

When it is winter in the Northern Hemisphere the north is tilted away from Sun.
The same radiation from the Sun

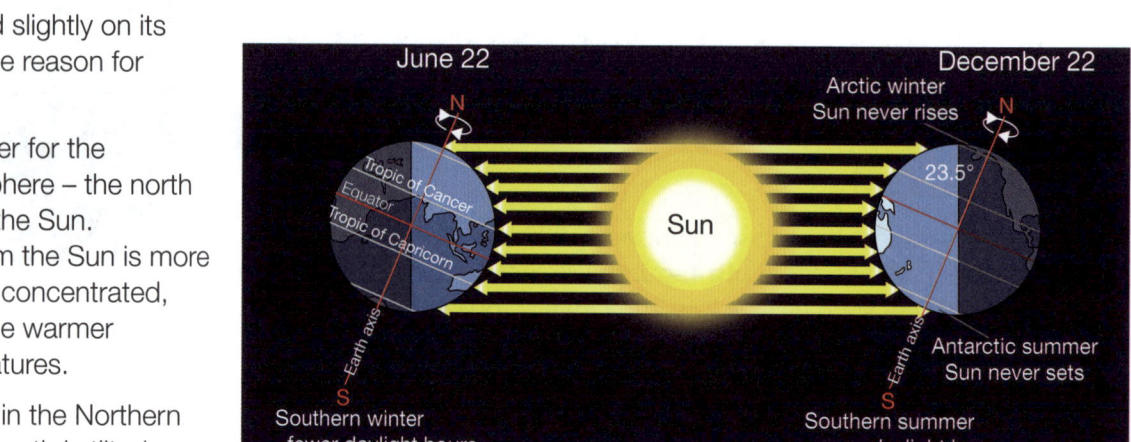

is spread over a larger area and has to travel through more of the atmosphere. Each part of the hemisphere receives less thermal energy and so we experience colder winter temperatures.

When it is summer in the Northern Hemisphere it is winter in the Southern Hemisphere, and vice versa.

- In the summer, we have long days and short nights. The summer solstice marks the start of summer, and is when the sun is highest in the sky. The summer solstice is the longest day of the year for that hemisphere.

- In winter, we have short days and long nights. The winter solstice marks the start of winter, and is when the sun is lowest in the sky. The winter solstice is the shortest day of the year for that hemisphere.

- An equinox is when day and night are equal length. We have an equinox in spring and autumn.

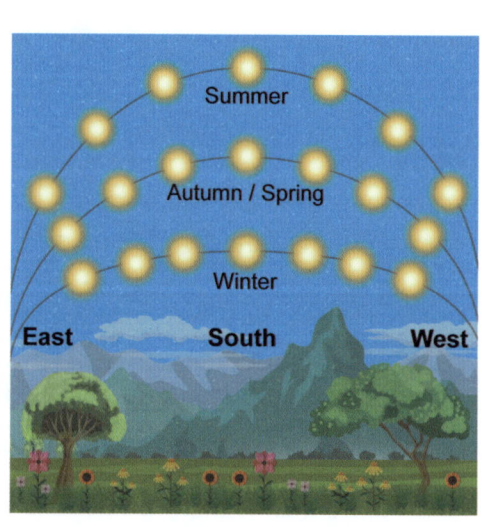

The Solar System

The Earth is one of 8 planets that orbit the Sun. The solar system also contains 5 dwarf planets, thousands of known comets, and millions of asteroids, which all orbit the Sun.

The gravitational pull of the Sun keeps everything in orbit around it. A solar system means the Sun and all the objects which orbit around it.

The Universe

Our Sun is a **star**. It is one of thousands of millions of stars in our **galaxy** called the Milky Way.

A galaxy is a collection of thousands of millions of stars. There are thought to be roughly 200 billion galaxies in our universe!

Astronomical distances are measured in **light years**. This is the distance light travels in one year.

one light year = 9.5 trillion km (9.46×10^{12} km)

The closest star to the Earth (after the Sun) is called Proxima Centauri, and it is 4.25 light years from Earth. This means when you are looking at the star, the light reaching your eyes is 4.25 years old.

Our nearest galaxy is the Andromeda galaxy which is over 2.5 million light years away. When you look at it through a telescope, you see it as it looked 2.5 million years ago.

✓ Check

1. If the Northern Hemisphere is tilted towards the Sun, what season is it in:
    a. The northern hemisphere? _____
    b. The southern hemisphere? _____
2. At what time of year is:
    a. The sun highest in the sky at midday? _____
    b. The sun lowest in the sky at midday? _____
3. What is the special name we give to:
    a. The longest day of the year? _____
    b. The shortest day of the year? _____
    c. The days when the length of day and night is the same? _____
4. What is meant by a 'light year'? _____

Glossary

A

acid a solution with a pH lower than 7

activation energy the amount of energy that has to be available before a chemical reaction is able to take place

addiction the need to keep taking a drug

aerobic respiration the process by which living things use oxygen to release energy from their food

air resistance the force that acts in the opposite direction to an object moving through the air

alkali a base that dissolves in water, forming a solution with a pH greater than 7

alloy a substance made from two or more metals combined in a specific proportion

alveoli tiny air sacs in the lungs where gas exchange takes place (singular: alveolus)

ammeter an instrument to measure electric current

amplitude the maximum displacement (height) of a wave compared to a reference value

anaemia a disease caused by not eating enough iron or vitamin B12, where a person is pale and feels very tired

anaerobic respiration the process living things use to break down their food and release energy without using oxygen

antagonistic pair two muscles that pull in opposite directions to move a bone at a joint

anther the male part of a flower which produces pollen

antibiotic a chemical/medicine that kills some types of bacteria

asthma a condition which affects the lungs and makes breathing difficult

atom the smallest part of an element that retains the element's properties

atomic number the number of protons in the nucleus of an atom

B

base a substance that reacts with an acid and neutralises it

bioaccumulation the build-up of toxic material in a food chain

biodiversity the range of different species in an ecosystem, or the range of variation in a species

biomass organic matter (dead plants, animals, faeces) that is used for fuel (burnt)

bronchiole small tubes inside the lungs which carry air to the alveoli

Brownian motion the random movement of particles in a fluid (liquid or gas) due to collisions with other atoms and molecules in the fluid

C

carbohydrate nutrients found in foods such as starch and sugar which give you energy

carbon cycle the continuous movement of carbon into and out of the atmosphere, animals, plants and the ground

carpel the female parts of a flower

cartilage a very smooth substance found on the ends of bones which allows them to move over each other easily

catalyst a chemical that lowers the activation energy of a reaction without being used up in the process

cell wall the supporting wall around a plant cell, made from cellulose

ceramic a non-metallic solid that has been altered by heating

chemical energy the amount of energy stored in chemical bonds; it can be released during combustion or respiration

chemical reaction a change that makes a new substance

chlorophyll a green pigment found in plants which is needed for photosynthesis

chloroplast parts of a plant cell that carry out photosynthesis

chromatography a method used to separate mixtures of substances based on their solubility

chromosome a long, coiled strand of DNA

cilia tiny hair-like structures that line the surfaces of some cells and help them move mucus

combustion the chemical reaction between a fuel and oxygen

compete living things trying to get the same resources as other organisms

composite a material made from two or more substances with different properties

compound a substance that contains more than one type of atom chemically joined together

compress to reduce the volume of a gas or liquid by applying pressure

conduction the flow of electrical or thermal energy through a material

conductor a material that allows thermal or electrical energy to easily pass through it

conservation protecting Earth's natural resources for current and future generations

consumer an animal which eats plants or animals to obtain energy

continuous variation variation which takes place across a range of values, such as height or weight

convex lens a lens which is thickest in the middle

crust the outermost layer of the Earth

cytoplasm the place where chemical reactions take place inside a cell

D

decomposers bacteria and fungi which break down dead organisms

density the amount of mass per unit volume of a material

diaphragm a dome-shaped sheet of muscle used during breathing

diffusion (biology) movement of molecules from an area of high to an area of low concentration (chemistry) particles of a gas or liquid spreading out as their particles move and mix

digestion process by which food is broken down into smaller molecules

discontinuous variation differences in features that have distinct groups, such as eye colour

dispersal the natural process by which seeds or pollen are spread or moved over a large area

displacement when a more reactive metal pushes out a less reactive metal from its compound in a reaction

dissolve when a solute is added to a solvent and the solute disappears

distillation a method used to separate mixtures of liquids with different boiling points

DNA the chemical that genes are made from

drag a force which acts against the movement of an object as it moves through a fluid (air or a liquid).

drug a chemical substance that affects the body

ductile able to be drawn out into a thin wire

E

echo a sound wave reflected off a surface

ecosystem a system of interacting organisms living in one area

egg cell female sex cell used for reproduction in plants and animals

electric current the flow of charge (negative electrons) around a circuit

electric field a field generated by electrically charged particles in a varying magnetic field

electromagnet a temporary magnet created by passing an electric current through a coiled wire

element a substance made up of only one type of atom

endangered when there are very few individuals remaining of a species and it is at risk of becoming extinct

endothermic a type of chemical reaction which takes in energy from its surroundings

energy transfer when energy is transferred from one energy store to another

enzyme proteins that speed up chemical reactions inside the body, such as the breakdown of food in digestion (biological catalyst)

equilibrium when all the forces acting on an object are balanced

evaporate when a liquid turns into a gas

evolution the gradual change of a species over time, because of natural selection

exothermic a type of chemical reaction which releases energy to its surroundings

extinct when a species has died out and completely disappeared from the Earth

F

fat a type of nutrient that contains lots of energy

fermentation the process of anaerobic respiration in yeast which produces ethanol

fertilisation the joining together of a male and female sex cell

fibre indigestible material found in food which helps nutrients move through the digestive system

Glossary

food chain a diagram which shows which organisms eat each other

food web food chains linked together to show the feeding relationship in an ecosystem

force a push or a pull resulting from the interactions between two objects

fossil fuels fuel produced from animals and plants that have been buried deep underground for millions of years

freeze when a liquid turns into a solid

frequency the number of waves that pass by a certain point per second (measured in Hz)

friction a force produced when two things rub together

fruit forms from a fertilised flower ovary; it contains the seed

G

galaxy a collection of millions of stars held together by gravitational pull

gas exchange the process of taking in oxygen and getting rid of carbon dioxide to maintain the body's breathing

gene the DNA instruction for one characteristic

gene bank a store of the genes of different species; it contains sperm, eggs and/or seeds

gestation the time from fertilisation to birth when a baby develops inside its mother

global warming the increase in the Earth's average temperature

glucose a sugar produced by photosynthesis

gravitational potential energy the amount of energy an object has due to its position in a gravitational field; the higher an object, the more energy it has

gravity the pulling force between one object and another; the force that pulls everything to the centre of the Earth and keeps the planets orbiting the Sun

greenhouse gases gases in the Earth's atmosphere that trap heat

group a column of elements in the periodic table

H

heredity characteristics being passed from one generation to the next

hydrocarbon a chemical compound that only contains the elements hydrogen and carbon

I

indicator a substance that shows whether a solution is acidic or alkaline by changing colour

inherited characteristics passed from one generation to the next

insoluble a substance that will not dissolve

insulator a material that does not conduct electrical or thermal energy

interdependent how organisms depend upon each other for survival

J

joint where two bones meet and can move

joule the unit of energy

K

kinetic energy the energy an object has due to its motion

L

lactic acid the waste substance produced by anaerobic respiration

lava magma that flows to the Earth's surface and escapes through a volcano or a fissure in the rock

law of conservation of energy energy cannot be created or destroyed, but it can be transferred from one energy store to another

law of reflection the angle of incidence of a light ray is equal to the angle of reflection

lever a simple machine that uses a pivot to make it easier to move heavy objects

ligament tissue that joins two bones together at a joint

light year the distance that light travels in one Earth year

longitudinal a wave in which the particles vibrate in the direction of travel

M

magma hot liquid rock formed under the Earth's crust

magnetic field the area around a magnet where it can affect other magnetic materials

magnet an object that has a magnetic field

malleable a material capable of being hammered into different shapes without breaking

mantle semi-solid layer inside the Earth made from molten rock

medicine a drug used to prevent or treat a disease

melt when a solid turns into a liquid

membrane the boundary of a cell that controls what goes into and out of the cell

menstrual cycle a monthly cycle in women; during the cycle, an egg is released and the woman has a period

minerals nutrients needed by our body in small quantities

mitochondria the part of a cell where respiration takes place

molecule a group of two or more atoms joined together

moment the turning effect of a force around a pivot, calculated by the force multiplied by the distance to the pivot

monomer a building block of a polymer

multicellular a living thing that is made up of more than one cell

N

natural selection the process where species that are better suited to their environment survive and pass on their traits to their offspring

neutral a chemical that is neither an acid nor a base, with pH 7

neutralisation the process where an acid is neutralised by a base, resulting in a solution with pH 7

newton the unit of force

non-renewable a kind of energy resource that will run out, for example, fossil fuels

nucleus the part of a cell which contains the DNA; it controls the cell

O

offspring new organisms produced by a living thing

ore a rock that contains enough metal to make extracting the metal for profit worthwhile

organ a group of different tissues that work together

organ system a group of organs that work together

organism a living thing

ovary the place where female sex cells (eggs) are made

ovulation when an egg is released from one of the ovaries during the menstrual cycle

oxidation when a chemical gains oxygen during a chemical reaction

oxygen a non-metallic, gaseous element, used in respiration and combustion; it is released by plants during photosynthesis

P

palisade cells the cells in a leaf where most photosynthesis takes place

peak the top of a wave (also called the crest)

period (chemistry) a horizontal row on the periodic table

pH scale a scale used to measure the strength of acidity or alkalinity

phloem tubes in a plant that carry water away from the leaves

photosynthesis the process by which plants make food (glucose)

physical change a change in which no new substance is made, such as in a change of state; can be easily reversed

pitch how high or low a sound is

pivot the point around which a lever turns

pollination the transfer of pollen from the anther of one flower to the stigma of another, either by insects or wind

polymer a long molecule made from a long chain of many monomers joined together

potential difference (p.d.) the difference in electrical potential between two points in a circuit; the size of the 'push' from the battery

power rating the amount of energy transferred each second by an appliance

pressure the effect of a force spread out over an area

producer an organism that produces its own food by photosynthesis

product substances produced by a chemical reaction

protein a nutrient used by the body for growth and repair

R

radiation when energy is transferred as a wave, such as light or sound

reactant substances in a chemical reaction that are changed by it

recycle reuse materials and make new items

reduction the loss of oxygen from a molecule

reflection the bouncing of light from a surface

Glossary

refraction the bending of light as it moves from one medium to another

relative motion how the motion of an object appears, depending on the position of the observer

renewable an energy resource that does not run out, such as wind or solar energy

resistance a measure of how difficult it is for current to flow through a component (measured in ohms)

respiration breaking down food to release energy

reversible capable of being reversed to a previous state

rickets a disease that affects how bones develop in children, caused by a lack of vitamin D

S

scurvy a disease caused by a lack of vitamin C

side effect an unwanted effect of a drug on the body

species a group of organisms that can reproduce to produce fertile offspring

speed the distance an object travels divided by the time travelled

sperm cell the male sex cell used for reproduction in animals

stamen the male part of a flower that produces pollen

star a hot ball of burning gas, held together by gravity

state (of matter) the physical form that a substance is in, such as solid, liquid or gas

stigma the female part of a flower where pollen is collected

stomata pots of small holes in the underside of a leaf (singular: stoma)

style long, tube-like structure in a flower, leading to the ovary

sublimation when a substance changes state from a solid to a gas without becoming a liquid

superposition where two waves meet and briefly add together

T

tendon tissue that attaches muscle to bone

testes place where sperm are made

thermal decomposition breakdown of a compound into products when heated

thermal equilibrium when two objects are the same temperature so no overall heat energy is transferred between them

tissue a group of the same type of cells

trachea a tube that leads from the mouth to the lungs, also called the windpipe

transverse a wave in which the particles vibrate at right angles to the direction of travel, such as light waves

trough the lowest part of a wave

U

ultrasound sound that is too high for a human ear to hear, typically over 20 000 Hz

unicellular an organism that consists of just one cell

upthrust the upwards reaction force of water pushing up against an object floating in it

uterus place where a baby grows

V

vaccination making the body produce antibodies to fight infection

vacuole storage place inside a plant cell; contains liquid to keep the cell firm

vagina muscular tube part of the female genital tract

variation differences between different organisms

vibration the movement of an object back and forth from a position of equilibrium

villi finger-like structures inside the small intestine which increase the surface area for absorption

vitamin essential nutrients needed in small amounts by the body

voltmeter an instrument used to measure voltage

volume amount of space occupied by an object or substance

W

wave a way that energy is transferred from one place to another

wavelength the distance from a point on one wave to the corresponding point on the next wave

weight the force of a mass in a gravitational field

X

xylem tubes in a plant that carry water and minerals from the roots to the leaf

Answers

BIOLOGY

Page 6 Cells
1. Any two from: cell wall, chloroplast(s), vacuole
2. a. nucleus
   b. mitochondria
   c. cell membrane
3. high, low

Page 7 Unicellular and Multicellular Organisms
1. flagellum to help them swim
2. a. tissue
   b. organ system
3. a. eyepiece (lens)
   b. stage

Page 8 Human Reproduction
1. a. testes
   b. sperm ducts
2. a. ovary/ovaries
   b. uterus (womb)
3. food, oxygen
4. a. day 1
   b. day 4
   c. day 14

Page 10 Respiration
1. glucose
2. mitochondria
3. carbon dioxide, water
4. a. carbon dioxide, alcohol
   b. fermentation

Page 12 Breathing and Gas Exchange
1. Breathing in: **Diaphragm** – Flattens downwards, **Movement of air** – Into lungs
   Breathing out: **Ribs** – Move down and out, **Volume of chest** – Decreases
2. moist, thin, good blood supply, large surface area
3. increase number of alveoli, increase number/size of blood vessels
4. diffusion (allow gas exchange)

Page 14 Diet and Digestion
1. enzymes
2. to kill bacteria, good pH for enzymes
3. Any six from: carbohydrates, protein, fat, vitamins, minerals, fibre, water
4. large surface area

Page 16 Skeleton, Muscles and Joints
1. supports the body/gives it structure, framework for muscles (moving), protects organs, makes blood cells
2. ligament
3. tendon
4. bone marrow

Page 18 Health and Drugs
1. unwanted effect of a drug (unpleasant, dangerous)
2. Any two from: strokes, heart disease, heart attacks, cancer, lung damage
3. becomes hard to stop taking the drug
4. damage liver, damage brain, strokes, heart attacks

Page 20 Plants and Photosynthesis
1. carbon dioxide + water → glucose + oxygen
2. Waxy layer – Stops plant losing water; Vein – Transports water to the leaf. Takes glucose away; Stomata – Lets gases in and out / lets oxygen out and carbon dioxide in; Palisade cells – Where most of the photosynthesis takes place in a leaf. Has lots of chloroplasts.
3. produces the oxygen that we breathe, produces our food (sugars and starches)

Page 22 Plant Reproduction
1. a. anther
   b. ovary
   c. stigma
2. Any two from: bright petals, nectar, smell
3. Any three from: wind, water, animals, drop and roll

Page 24 Relationships in an Ecosystem
1. It uses the Sun to make food / traps energy from Sun
2. direction of energy flow
3. a. grass
   b. rabbit and fox
   c. fox
   d. bioaccumulation

Page 26 DNA and Inheritance
1. 46 (23 pairs)
2. 23
3. heredity
4. DNA
5. gene

Page 28 Variation Between Organisms
1. receiving a mixture of genes from our parents
2. Continuous: Any valid, e.g. height, weight, foot length, leaf area, hand span
   Discontinuous: Any valid, e.g. blood group, eye colour, tongue roller
3. Any environmental reason, e.g. different diet, exercise, changed hair colour, accident, disease, surgery

Page 30 Natural Selection and Biodiversity
1. the range of different organisms in a habitat
2. a. sperm and eggs
   b. seeds
3. natural selection
4. all of a species die out

Answers

CHEMISTRY

Page 32 Solids, Liquids, Gases and the Particle Model
1. particles are much closer together
2.

	Solid	Liquid	Gas
Fixed shape?	Yes	No	No
Can squash?	No	No	Yes
Can pour?	No	Yes	Yes

3. a. solid
   b. gas
   c. liquid

Page 34 Physical Changes
1. 0°C
2. 100°C
3. a. melting, boiling/evaporation
   b. freezing, condensing
4. sublimation

Page 35 Atoms and Elements
1. elements
2. compound
3. molecule
4. hydrogen, oxygen

Page 36 Mixing and Moving Particles
1. 220g
2. use hotter water, stir it, use finer sugar
3. high, low, diffusion
4. Brownian motion

Page 38 Separating Mixtures
1. a. filtration
   b. chromatography
   c. evaporation
2. grinding, dissolving, filtering, evaporating
3. contains no other substances in it

Page 40 The Periodic Table
1. soft, shiny, reacts with water
2. less reactive
3. non-metal
4. carbon, four

Page 42 Types of Chemical Reaction
1. a. oxidation
   b. copper oxide
   c. copper + oxygen → copper oxide
2. metal oxide, carbon dioxide
3. fuel, oxygen, heat

Page 44 Metals and Non-metals
1. Shiny – metal; Brittle – non-metal; Electrical insulator – non-metal; Good conductor of heat – metal; Malleable – metal; Gas at room temperature – non-metal
2. alloy
3. Any three from: iron, cobalt, nickel, steel

Page 46 Endothermic and Exothermic Reactions
1. absorb/take in, give off, colder, warmer
2. speed it up
3. a. exothermic
   b. exothermic
   c. endothermic
   d. endothermic

Page 48 Acids and Bases
1. a. a base/alkali
   b. neutralisation
2. a. sodium nitrate + water
   b. calcium chloride + water + carbon dioxide
3. a. red
   b. pink
   c. bright red

Page 50 Metals and the Reactivity Series
1. a. no
   b. yes
   c. yes
2. a. Z
   b. X
   c. Y
3. more/most, less, displacement

Page 52 Metals and Ores
1. copper, zinc
2. iron, reactive
3. carbon dioxide + iron

Page 53 Other Useful Materials
1. (good) insulator
2. a. sand, small stones
   b. makes it stronger
3. monomers

Page 54 The Earth and Rocks
1. Igneous rock with large crystals, e.g. Granite: with small crystals, e.g. Basalt;
2. crust, mantle, core
3. oxygen
4. a. igneous
   b. metamorphic
   c. sedimentary

Page 56 Carbon and the Climate
1. a. photosynthesis
   b. Any two from: burning fossil fuels, respiration, decomposing
2. burning lots of fossil fuels, deforestation
3. greenhouse, heat/energy, atmosphere, warming

Answers

PHYSICS

Page 58 Forces
1. a. balanced
   b. unbalanced
2. 200 N to the left
3. 200 N × 3 m = 600 Nm

Page 60 Speed and Relative Motion
1. 100 km/h
2. a. object is stationary
   b. moving away at steady speed
   c. moving closer at steady speed
   d. accelerating and moving away
3. a. 90 m/s
   b. 10 m/s

Page 62 Friction and Drag
1. a. slower
   b. faster
2. to reduce air resistance
3. On the Moon there is no air resistance to slow down the feather.

Page 63 Forces and Elasticity
1. extension, proportional, force
2. a. 6 cm
   b. 10 cm
3. joule/J (or kilojoule kJ)
4. equilibrium

Page 64 Pressure

Force	Area	Pressure
30 N	5 m²	6 N/m²
68 N	2 m²	34 N/m²
50 N	10 m²	5 N/m²
8 N	4 m²	2 N/m²
20 N	40 m²	0.5 N/m²

2. 800 N
3. Larger pressure. Because more water is pressing down on them.

Page 66 Non-contact Forces
1. a. 600 N
   b. less
   c. gravitational pull (gravity) is less on the Moon
2. a. repel
   b. attract
   c. attract
   d. repel
3. non-contact forces
4. Any three from: static electricity, magnetism, gravity, electric fields

Page 68 Energy Stores and Energy Transfers
1. created, destroyed, transferred, (energy) store
2. mechanically, heating, electrically, radiation
3. a. kinetic
   b. gravitational
   c. chemical
   d. elastic

Page 70 Work and Machines
1. joule or kilojoule
2. work done = force × distance
3. a. 1800 J
   b. 600 J
   c. 1000 J

Page 71 Transferring Thermal Energy
1. a. conduction
   b. radiation
2. hotter, cooler
3. thermal equilibrium
4. a. any metal
   b. any plastic, ceramics

Page 72 Fuels and Energy Resources
1. carbohydrates, fats, proteins
2. fossil fuel
3. solar, wind, wave (also biomass, food)
4. a. 6 kWh
   b. 90p

Page 74 Electrical Circuits
1. charge/electrons
2. potential difference
3. ohms
4. current
5. 0.1 Ω

Page 76 Magnets and Electromagnets
1. larger current, coil the wire, use a core made from magnetic material
2. increase the current, use stronger magnets
3. iron, nickel

Page 78 Properties of Waves
1. A = peak/crest; B = trough; C = wavelength; D = amplitude
2. a. they add together/get higher
   b. they add together/get deeper
   c. they cancel each other out/flatten out
3. ripple tank
4. light

Page 80 Light Waves
1. focus light onto the retina
2. angle of incidence is equal to angle of reflection
3. a. more dense, towards
   b. less dense, away
   c. refraction

Page 82 Sound Waves
1. a. solid
   b. gas/air
2. a vacuum
3. pitch gets higher

Page 84 Earth and Space
1. a. summer
   b. winter
2. a. summer
   b. winter
3. a. summer solstice
   b. winter solstice
   c. equinox
4. the distance light travels in one year

Progress Tracker

	Revised	Checked
Biology		
Cells		
Unicellular and Multicellular Organisms		
Human Reproduction		
Respiration		
Breathing and Gas Exchange		
Diet and Digestion		
Skeleton, Muscles and Joints		
Health and Drugs		
Plants and Photosynthesis		
Plant Reproduction		
Relationships in an Ecosystem		
DNA and Inheritance		
Variation Between Organisms		
Natural Selection and Biodiversity		

	Revised	Checked
Physics		
Forces		
Speed and Relative Motion		
Friction and Drag		
Forces and Elasticity		
Pressure		
Non-contact Forces		
Energy Stores and Energy Transfers		
Work and Machines		
Transferring Thermal Energy		
Fuels and Energy Resources		
Electrical Circuits		
Magnets and Electromagnets		
Properties of Waves		
Light Waves		
Sound Waves		
Earth and Space		

	Revised	Checked
Chemistry		
Solids, Liquids, Gases and the Particle Model		
Physical Changes		
Atoms and Elements		
Mixing and Moving Particles		
Separating Mixtures		
The Periodic Table		
Types of Chemical Reaction		
Metals and Non-metals		
Endothermic and Exothermic Reactions		
Acids and Bases		
Metals and the Reactivity Series		
Metals and Ores		
Other Useful Materials		
The Earth and Rocks		
Carbon and the Climate		

Notes

SCHOLASTIC

10-Minute Tests

Quick tests for success

- Make sure you understand the essential concepts and skills
- Identify where you need to revise and study more
- Track improvement with the progress tracker
- Answers included

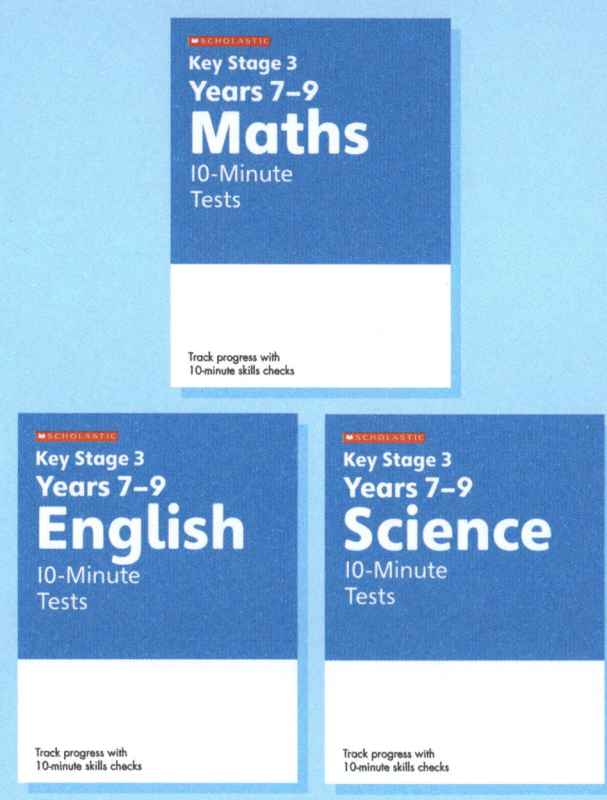

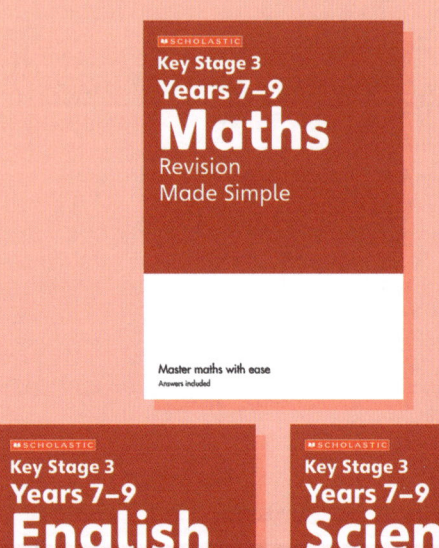

Made Simple

Recap, revise and check key concepts

- Full subject coverage
- Recap existing knowledge and revise new learning
- Practice questions are included to check understanding
- Answers included

Available at **WHSmith** EST·1792